GCSE
Success

WORKBOOK

English Language & Literature

Paul Burns

Contents

Back to Basics

Multiple-choice questions

Choose just one answer: A, B, C or D.

1 Choose the sentence in which commas are used correctly. **(1 mark)**
A I left the house, I had to go to the shops.
B Romeo fell in love with Juliet, she was the prettiest girl he had ever seen.
C Juliet, who was the prettiest girl in Verona, fell in love with Romeo.
D In the shop I bought oranges, and apples, and bananas.

2 Choose the sentence in which both a question mark and inverted commas (speech marks) are used correctly. **(1 mark)**
A Caroline asked Peter 'if he had everything he needed?'
B 'Have you got everything you need, Peter?' asked Caroline.
C 'Caroline' asked whether 'Peter' had everything he needed?
D 'Caroline asked Peter do you have everything you need?'

3 Choose the sentence in which the apostrophe is used correctly. **(1 mark)**
A The children's homework wasn't good enough.

B The childrens' homework wasnt good enough.
C The childrens homework wasn't good enough.
D The childrens' homework was'nt good enough.

4 Choose the sentence in which capital letters are used correctly. **(1 mark)**
A The smallest planet in the solar system is Mercury.
B the smallest Planet in the Solar System is Mercury.
C The shortest Month in the Year is February.
D The shortest month in the year is February.

5 Which of these sentences is grammatically correct? **(1 mark)**
A Stan and I was very unhappy about last Saturday's result.
B Me and Stan both scored on Saturday.
C The coach praised Stan and I after the match.
D Stan and I were both mentioned in the paper after Saturday's match.

Score / 5

Short-answer questions

The following passages contain neither punctuation nor capital letters. Write them out correctly on a separate sheet of paper. Award yourself up to five marks for each passage. **(10 marks)**

last monday kelly and ruksana were overjoyed when they heard justin bieber was in town unfortunately neither of them was able to get tickets for the concert just after lunch while kelly was at dance practice ruksana received a text from her friend elle it said that justin had just arrived at his hotel and elle was outside not only had she seen him she had taken a picture of him getting out of his car

can you come out tonight asked tom were going for a pizza im not sure jon replied mum wants me to go to nans its her sixtieth birthday that sounds like fun yeah plus she wants me to do the shopping ive got a massive list cake jellies sausage rolls chicken drumsticks and just about everything else

Score / 10

4

GCSE-style questions

Continue on a separate sheet of paper if necessary.

Focus on using a range of correct punctuation. When you have finished, check your work or ask someone to check it for you and mark it for technical accuracy.

Either

1 You have been asked to write an article for a school newspaper about a recent event in school. It could be a sports fixture, a musical or theatrical production, or a visit by a well-known person.   **(10 marks)**

The article should include:

- what the event was, and when and where it was held
- who was involved
- what happened
- how and why the event matters.

or

2 Describe a person you admire. It could be someone you know well or someone you have never met.   **(10 marks)**

You could include:

- what he or she looks and sounds like
- his or her personality and character
- things he or she has done
- what the person means to you.

Score   / 10

How well did you do?

| 0–9 | Try again | 10–14 | Getting there | 15–19 | Good work | 20–25 | Excellent! |

For more information on this topic, see pages 6–7 of your Success Revision Guide.

Writing Skills

Multiple-choice questions

Choose just one answer: A, B, C or D.

1 What must a simple sentence include? (1 mark)
- **A** A noun, a verb and an adjective.
- **B** A question mark.
- **C** A subject and a verb.
- **D** A subject, a verb and an object.

2 What does a compound sentence do? (1 mark)
- **A** It joins two or more clauses together using a conjunction.
- **B** It gives us information that we do not need.
- **C** It joins two or more clauses together with a comma.
- **D** It includes adverbs and adjectives.

3 What does a subordinate clause do? (1 mark)
- **A** It disagrees with the main clause.
- **B** It adds extra information to the main clause.
- **C** It tells us who is speaking.
- **D** It describes the scene.

4 When should you start a new paragraph? (1 mark)
- **A** When you get bored.
- **B** When you change topic, place or time.
- **C** When you get to the end of the page.
- **D** Three times on every page.

5 In which of the following is the conjunction 'however' used with the correct punctuation? (1 mark)
- **A** The cat was ill however it still ate its meal.
- **B** Cats are rarely ill. However you must never give your cat medicine without seeing a vet first.
- **C** My friend said I should give milk to the cat. The vet, however, said that milk was bad for cats.
- **D** I was quite worried when I went to the vet's, however it turned out that the cat was quite well.

Score   / 5

Short-answer questions

1 Change each of the following pairs of sentences into a single sentence using an appropriate conjunction. Award yourself one mark for each correct answer.   (5 marks)

- **a)** I stayed off school yesterday. I had a stomach ache.
- **b)** She might have gone to the supermarket. She could still be at work.
- **c)** My grandmother is over eighty. She still enjoys aerobics.
- **d)** The dog was scratching at the door. We let him out.
- **e)** We were really enjoying the programme. The dog spoilt it by barking at the television.

2 Rewrite the passage on the right on a separate sheet of paper, using a variety of simple, compound and complex sentences (and adding words where necessary) to make it more effective. Award yourself up to five marks.   (5 marks)

> I left work early that day. I had a headache. I was waiting at the bus stop. A woman stopped to talk to me. She was very tall. She had red hair. She came from Darlington. I was surprised. It is long way off. She had taken the wrong bus. Now she had to get home. She was at the wrong bus stop. I told her where to go. I offered to take her. She said she would be all right. She walked off in the wrong direction. I shouted to her. She did not turn round. She turned the corner. I ran after her. She had disappeared.

Score   / 10

GCSE-style questions

Continue on a separate sheet of paper if necessary.

Focus on using a range of correct punctuation and sentence structures, and using paragraphs. When you have finished, check your work or ask someone to check it for you and mark it for technical accuracy.

Either

1 Write a diary entry as if it were written by a character in a text that you have studied. You should try to describe events from the character's point of view and refer to his or her feelings about what happens. **(10 marks)**

or

2 Write a magazine article featuring an interview with another character in which you discuss that character's part in the events of the text. **(10 marks)**

or

3 Write a letter from the character to a close friend, explaining his or her actions. **(10 marks)**

Score / 10

How well did you do?

| 0–9 | Try again | 10–14 | Getting there | 15–19 | Good work | 20–25 | Excellent! |

For more information on this topic, see pages 8–9 of your Success Revision Guide.

Writing Skills

Multiple-choice questions

Choose just one answer: A, B, C or D.

For each of the sentences below, choose the one where all the words are spelled correctly.

1
 A On her way back from netball practise, Keira slipped and broke her ankle. (1 mark)
 B Remember to practice your spellings before the test.
 C Your playing will improve only if you practise every day.
 D Al was lucky to get a work-experiance placement at the chiropodist's practice.

2
 A Their not very happy with there accomodation. (1 mark)
 B They're not very happy with their accommodation.
 C There not very happy with there accommodation.
 D They're not very happy with their acomodation.

3
 A Where did you say you went yesterday? (1 mark)
 B Yesterday we where in Blackpool.
 C Did you ware your new coat or where you too hot?
 D Unfortunatly, it was very cold. It always is in Febuary.

4
 A Two many cooks spoil the broth. (1 mark)
 B I think too cooks is enough.
 C You need only one cook too make a broth.
 D Two might be too many then.

5
 A Is it really neccessary to make the test so difficult? (1 mark)
 B I hardly new any of the answers.
 C I no a lot about science but I still couldn't do it.
 D I knew some of it already but a lot of it was new to me.

Score / 5

Short-answer questions

All the highlighted words in the following passage are spelt incorrectly. Write out the passage correctly and give yourself one mark for each one you get right. Continue on a separate sheet of paper.

(10 marks)

Last **Wensday** I was supposed to be travelling to Spain to see my grandmother. However, while I was packing, I **herd** on the radio that there was very bad **whether** over France, as a result of **witch** all flights were subject to delay or even **cancelation**. I **paniced**. I just didn't know what to do – **weather** to go to the airport and hope for the best, or stay at home and try to rearrange my trip. I **new** my grandmother would be very **disapointed** if I didn't get **their**.

Score / 10

Continue on a separate sheet of paper if necessary.

Focus on using a range of correct punctuation and sentence structures, spelling correctly and using paragraphs. When you have finished, check your work or ask someone to check it for you and mark it for technical accuracy.

Either

1 Write a letter to a friend describing a place you visited last year and trying to persuade your friend to go there too. You should write in a friendly and informal tone. (10 marks)

or

2 Write a short review for a website about a holiday resort you have visited recently. The website is designed to be read by people of all ages. (10 marks)

Score / 10

How well did you do?

| 0–9 | Try again | 10–14 | Getting there | 15–19 | Good work | 20–25 | Excellent! |

For more information on this topic, see pages 10–11 of your Success Revision Guide.

Introduction

Reading Non-Fiction

Multiple-choice questions

Choose just one answer: A, B, C or D.

1 Which of the following is **not** an example of a non-fiction text? **(1 mark)**
A An encyclopedia.
B A website.
C A novel.
D A diary.

2 Which of the following are features of a newspaper report? **(1 mark)**
A A headline, a strapline and columns.
B Cartoons with speech bubbles and captions.
C Chapter headings.
D Rhyme, rhythm and imagery.

3 What do we call the story of someone's life written by himself or herself? **(1 mark)**
A A biography.
B An essay.
C A manual.
D An autobiography.

4 What does 'summarising' mean? **(1 mark)**
A Adding things up.
B Writing a shorter version of a text.
C Copying out a text.
D Writing a critical evaluation of a text.

5 When writing about a non-fiction text, it is important to be able to: **(1 mark)**
A distinguish between fact and opinion.
B write neatly.
C discuss the writer's life.
D agree with the writer's views.

Score / 5

Short-answer questions

What are the main purposes of the following non-fiction texts? Give yourself one mark for each correct answer, remembering that some of them may have more than one purpose.

1 recipes .... (1 mark)

2 advertisements .... (1 mark)

3 dictionaries .... (1 mark)

4 teenage magazines .... (1 mark)

5 travel writing .... (1 mark)

Score / 5

GCSE-style questions

Continue on a separate sheet of paper if necessary.

Read carefully the passage below, which is part of a tourist guide to Italy.

> Lake Garda is Italy's largest lake, a beautiful expanse of blue originally created by glaciation. The glorious surrounding scenery varies from dramatic snow-capped mountains to tranquil sandy shores and soft vine-covered hills. This area has inspired poets and painters from Roman times to the present day. Now Lake Garda is becoming one of Italy's most popular tourist destinations, an ideal spot for walking, water sports, or simply relaxing in the sun.
>
> One of its most attractive resorts is Sirmione. With a permanent population of just 5,100, this picturesque town is thronged with visitors throughout the season. However, it is still possible to find peaceful spots, where its Roman and medieval past comes alive. And, if you're not entranced by its history, you may find yourself seduced by its many top-class restaurants and luxurious hotels.

1 Write down two facts about Lake Garda. **(2 marks)**

Fact 1 ....

....

....

Fact 2 ....

....

....

2 The passage tries to persuade the reader to visit Lake Garda by painting a very positive picture of the area.

Identify three words that would help to achieve this, and briefly explain their effect on the reader.

Positive words about Lake Garda	The effect of each word on the reader
1 **(1 mark)**	**(2 marks)**
2 **(1 mark)**	**(2 marks)**
3 **(1 mark)**	**(2 marks)**

Score   / 11

How well did you do?

| 0–7 | Try again | 8–11 | Getting there | 12–15 | Good work | 16–21 | Excellent! |

For more information on this topic, see pages 12–13 of your Success Revision Guide.

Non-Fiction

Conventions and Features

Multiple-choice questions

Choose just one answer: A, B, C or D.

1 Adjectives are: **(1 mark)**
- **A** words that name things
- **B** words used to describe nouns
- **C** action words
- **D** words used to describe verbs.

2 Adverbs are: **(1 mark)**
- **A** words used to describe nouns
- **B** words that compare one thing to another
- **C** words that describe actions
- **D** words used to describe verbs.

3 Emotive language is used: **(1 mark)**
- **A** to trigger an emotional response in a reader
- **B** to describe an emotion
- **C** to amuse a reader
- **D** to impress a reader.

4 A connotation is: **(1 mark)**
- **A** the meaning of a word
- **B** the opposite of a word's meaning
- **C** an association carried by a word or symbol
- **D** a word used symbolically.

5 An anecdote is: **(1 mark)**
- **A** a joke
- **B** a short, usually humorous, story
- **C** a word with more than one meaning
- **D** a short newspaper article.

Score / 5

Short-answer questions

1 Five of the following terms refer to features of presentation and five to language features. Which are which? Give yourself half a point for each correct answer. **(5 marks)**

bullet points	imperative	oxymoron	metaphor	illustration
hyperbole	logo	subheading	assonance	bold font

Presentational Features	Linguistic Features

2 The passage on the right contains at least five features that are often found in non-fiction texts. How many can you name? Give yourself one mark for each feature correctly identified. Answer on a separate sheet of paper. **(5 marks)**

> If this proposal goes ahead, the effect on our lives could be disastrous. They will close our libraries, neglect our schools and destroy our health centres. What can you do to prevent this vandalism?
>
> Well, you could:
> - write a letter to your councillor
> - join a march to the town hall
> - vote for us at the next election.
>
> Stop this vandalism now!

Score / 10

Continue on a separate sheet of paper if necessary.

Read the following text, which is taken from an advertisement appealing for money for the Royal National Lifeboat Institution (RNLI), and answer both the questions below.

1 How does the writer use language to inform readers about the work of the RNLI? Use examples from the text to support your answer.   **(5 marks)**

....
....
....
....
....
....

2 How does the writer use language to persuade readers to leave money to the RNLI? Use examples from the text to support your answer.   **(5 marks)**

....
....
....
....
....
....

Courage
is timeless

TIME MARCHES ON. Society transforms faster than we can keep up with it. But the bravery of the RNLI's lifeboat crews has been steadfast for over 185 years. Thank goodness – because for all the advantages new technology brings, the sea remains a dangerous place. Conditions change in the blink of an eye and when sailors find themselves in trouble, the RNLI is there. Last year alone our lifeboats aided over 8,000 people: but without the caring and responsible members of the public who support our work, we couldn't exist at all.

Celebrating our past

To celebrate and commemorate all that our lifeboat crews have achieved we've put together a free booklet, *Courage is timeless* – you can request your copy simply by returning the coupon or calling the number below. Of course, all the acts of bravery by RNLI crew you'll read about, are only possible because the public are kind enough to recognise the importance of our work, and support us in it.

Your part in our future

One of the best ways to support those courageous and selfless lifeboatmen and women, who volunteer to save others, is by remembering the RNLI in your Will. Six out of ten of all lifeboat launches have only been possible because kind people had the foresight to leave us a gift. All it takes is a small change to your Will. And even a small gift will help us achieve so much. With your support, we'll always be here for those in peril on the sea.

If you would like to receive a legacy information pack which includes a copy of *Courage is timeless*, please return the coupon below or alternatively visit our website, rnli.org.uk/legacy.

Lifeboats

REMEMBER THE RNLI IN YOUR WILL
Help the work live on...

Registered in England and Wales (209603) and Scotland (SC037736). Charity number CHY 2678 in the Republic of Ireland

☐ **Please send me a legacy information pack.**

Please return this form to: Mark Allwood, Legacy Enquiries Manager, RNLI, FREEPOST (BH173), West Quay Road, Poole, Dorset, BH15 1BF.

TITLE _____ FORENAME _____

SURNAME _____

ADDRESS _____

_____ POSTCODE _____

We never give your information to other organisations for marketing purposes. Your details will be used by the RNLI and passed to RNLI trading companies. We would only give your data to another organisation if required to do so by law. If you do not want to receive information about other ways to support the RNLI, please tick here ☐ DPA

RT03/11CIT

FundRaising Standards Board

Call Mark Allwood on 01202 663032 or email: mark_allwood@rnli.org.uk

Thank you

Score / 10

How well did you do?

0–9 | Try again   **10–14** | Getting there   **15–19** | Good work   **20–25** | Excellent!

For more information on this topic, see pages 14–15 of your Success Revision Guide.

Writing Techniques

Multiple-choice questions

Choose just one answer: A, B, C or D.

1 A fact is: **(1 mark)**
- **A** a statement that you agree with
- **B** something that can be proven to be true
- **C** a statistic
- **D** something you have read about.

2 An opinion is: **(1 mark)**
- **A** what somebody thinks about something
- **B** something you do not believe
- **C** something that everybody agrees with
- **D** an offensive remark.

3 Non-fiction texts often include quotations from experts to: **(1 mark)**
- **A** make the text more amusing
- **B** show off the writer's knowledge

- **C** confuse the reader
- **D** back up the writer's opinions and make them seem more credible.

4 Anecdotes are used to: **(1 mark)**
- **A** make the text seem more personal and entertain the reader
- **B** give extra factual information
- **C** deceive the reader
- **D** explain difficult ideas in simple language.

5 Rhetoric is: **(1 mark)**
- **A** the art of persuasive speaking or writing
- **B** the science of persuasive speaking or writing
- **C** the art of lying
- **D** speaking very loudly and slowly.

Score / 5

Short-answer questions

For each of the following examples, state whether it is presented as a fact or an opinion and give a reason for your answer.

1 According to the latest census, over 20 per cent of people in the city live alone. **(2 marks)**

2 I am convinced that the exploitation of our resources in this way is not only irresponsible, but is also morally wrong. **(2 marks)**

3 In the twenty-first century nobody should have to live in these conditions. Everybody is entitled to a comfortable home and enough money to be able to enjoy their old age. **(2 marks)**

4 Liechtenstein is one of the smallest sovereign states in Europe, with an area of approximately 160 square metres and a population of 35,000. Its capital is Vaduz. **(2 marks)**

5 Local resident, Mrs Elsie Arbuthnot, told me that, since the new road was built, the neighbourhood has 'gone right down' and she and many others like her feel that life in the village is becoming a nightmare, 'like something out of a horror story'. **(2 marks)**

Score / 10

Continue on a separate sheet of paper if necessary.

Read the newspaper article below ('Yasha, 8, Is Sum Genius!').

March 20, 2011

YASHA, 8, IS SUM GENIUS!

He gets A for A-level maths

BOY genius Yasha Ayari Asley is sum-thing special – he passed A-level maths with an A at the age of EIGHT.

Yasha is the youngest person ever to score the grade in all SIX modules of the super-hard exam. But remarkably he was in tears after failing to score 100 per cent in them all.

Whizkid Yasha had already stunned the world by passing one module last year, aged SEVEN.

But now he's passed the lot to become Britain's youngest maths genius.

Yasha, who attends a state primary school in Leicester and has 30 pupils in his class, was still frustrated. He said: "It was annoying because on some papers I ran out of time. I wanted to get 100 per cent. I knew all the answers but there wasn't enough time." Yasha sat six papers over three days at the City of Leicester College in January, enduring two exams each day.

Yasha did manage one 100 per cent score. And in another paper he got 99 per cent. Proud dad Moussa, 48, said: "In one exam he cried because he was so upset at not having enough time. It's tough for him as he's not been expertly tutored. He taught himself everything. But what he has achieved is remarkable."

By DOUGLAS WIGHT

❶ List five pieces of information that the article tells you about Yasha Asley.   **(5 marks)**

....

....

....

....

....

....

❷ Why do you think that Wight refers to him as a 'genius'?   **(5 marks)**

....

....

....

....

Score   / 10

How well did you do?

| 0–9 | Try again | 10–14 | Getting there | 15–19 | Good work | 20–25 | Excellent! |

For more information on this topic, see pages 16–17 of your Success Revision Guide.

Non-Fiction

Audience

Multiple-choice questions

Choose just one answer: A, B, C or D.

For each of the following definitions, select the correct term.

1 A newspaper, traditionally larger in size, which takes a more serious approach to the news: **(1 mark)**
- A tabloid
- B magazine
- C editorial
- D broadsheet.

2 A subheading, under the main headline, that expands on or helps to explain the headline: **(1 mark)**
- A strapline
- B subline
- C byline
- D underline.

3 A subheading that identifies the writer of the article: **(1 mark)**
- A strapline
- B byline
- C name check
- D nameline.

4 The people at whom a text is aimed: **(1 mark)**
- A target audience
- B general public
- C target people
- D focus group.

5 Making assumptions about people according to whether they are male or female: **(1 mark)**
- A racial stereotyping
- B sexual orientation
- C gender stereotyping
- D social sex-typing.

Score / 5

Short-answer questions

The terms below refer to typical features of tabloid and/or broadsheet newspapers. Under each heading list the features you would expect to find, remembering that some might appear in both lists. (10 marks)

- a) masthead
- b) celebrity gossip
- c) horoscopes
- d) sophisticated vocabulary
- e) pictures of glamour models
- f) news reports
- g) long and detailed reports on foreign affairs
- h) very short paragraphs
- i) leaders (or editorials)
- j) reviews
- k) letters to the editor
- l) cartoons
- m) sports reports
- n) contrasting opinion pieces

Tabloids	Broadsheets

Score / 10

Continue on a separate sheet of paper if necessary.

Look again at the article on page 15 ('Yasha, 8, Is Sum Genius!').

How does Douglas Wight try to make his newspaper article interesting for readers?   **(10 marks)**

Think about:

- what he says
- how he says it
- the use of headlines and sub-headings
- the use of other presentational devices.

Score   / 10

How well did you do?

| 0–9 | Try again | 10–14 | Getting there | 15–19 | Good work | 20–25 | Excellent! |

For more information on this topic, see pages 18–19 of your Success Revision Guide.

Writing Non-Fiction

Multiple-choice questions

Choose just one answer: A, B, C or D.

1 Why is it important to check how many marks are awarded for each part of an exam question? **(1 mark)**
- **A** It helps you to plan how long you spend on each part.
- **B** It tells you how many words to include in your answer.
- **C** It helps you decide which part to answer.
- **D** It makes no difference whatsoever.

2 How does making a plan help to improve your marks? **(1 mark)**
- **A** If it looks good the examiner will give you extra marks.
- **B** It means you do not have to worry about writing in paragraphs.
- **C** It helps you to structure your piece and organise your time.
- **D** It will give you a chance to use lots of different coloured pens.

3 How long should you spend planning a question for which you are given an hour? **(1 mark)**
- **A** About a minute
- **B** About five minutes
- **C** About fifteen minutes
- **D** About half an hour.

4 Which of these do you **not** need to think about when writing your answer? **(1 mark)**
- **A** Its purpose
- **B** The intended audience
- **C** The appropriate tone
- **D** The question you answered in your mock exam.

5 What should you allow time to do when you have finished writing your answer? **(1 mark)**
- **A** Write a little note to the examiner.
- **B** Illustrate your work.
- **C** Write it all out again neatly.
- **D** Check paragraphing, punctuation and spelling.

Score   / 5

Short-answer questions

1 What are the purposes of the following types of writing? Give yourself one mark for each correct answer. Bear in mind that they may have more than one purpose. Continue on a separate sheet of paper.

a) A user's manual for a new car. .... (1 mark)

b) A flyer from a charity asking for donations. .... (1 mark)

c) An article in a travel magazine about the writer's trip to Bali. .... (1 mark)

d) An opinion piece in a broadsheet. .... (1 mark)

2 At what audiences do you think the following publications are primarily aimed?

a) *Vogue* .... (1 mark)

b) *The Beano* .... (1 mark)

c) *The Sunday Times* .... (1 mark)

d) *Farmers' Weekly* .... (1 mark)

Score   / 8

GCSE-style questions

You will see that these questions require you to write for very different audiences. Continue on a separate sheet of paper if necessary.

You will be assessed for your writing skills, including the presentation of your work. Take special care with handwriting, spelling and punctuation.

Think about the purpose, audience and, where appropriate, the format of your writing.

Either

❶ You have seen an advertisement in the local paper for a new fast food restaurant, which is opening in your area and is looking for part-time staff. The advertisement invites suitable candidates to write to Ms Jayne Frobisher, the Human Resources Manager. Write a letter of application. **(20 marks)**

or

❷ You are thinking about a career in teaching infants. However, before you decide which A levels to do, you want to be sure it is the right career for you. Write to the head teacher of your old primary school, asking him or her if you can visit for a day to observe lessons. **(20 marks)**

Score / 20

How well did you do?

| 0–11 | Try again | 12–18 | Getting there | 19–25 | Good work | 26–33 | Excellent! |

For more information on this topic, see pages 20–21 of your Success Revision Guide.

Writing for Different Audiences

Multiple-choice questions

Choose just one answer: A, B, C or D.

1 What is Standard English? **(1 mark)**
- **A** The language used in the south of England.
- **B** English that is very difficult to understand.
- **C** Written English.
- **D** English that is universally recognised as such and considered correct.

2 In which of the following would it be acceptable for you **not** to use Standard English? **(1 mark)**
- **A** A leading article for a newspaper.
- **B** An article for a teenage magazine.
- **C** A letter to your Member of Parliament.
- **D** An instruction manual for a washing machine.

3 What is dialect? **(1 mark)**
- **A** The way people pronounce their words.
- **B** A regional variation of English.
- **C** Slang.
- **D** A conversation between two people.

4 What is meant by colloquial language? **(1 mark)**
- **A** Informal language of the kind used in everyday speech.
- **B** Language that other people might find offensive.
- **C** Language used in scientific texts.
- **D** French.

5 If you are writing a letter that begins 'Dear Sir' or 'Dear Madam', how should it end? **(1 mark)**
- **A** Lots of love...
- **B** Yours sincerely...
- **C** Yours faithfully...
- **D** Yours truly...

Score / 5

Short-answer questions

Rewrite the following letter using Standard English. Write your answer on a separate sheet of paper.

(10 marks)

> Hi Banksy,
>
> Me and the other pupils are well cheesed off about what's been going down in school lately. All this biz about school uniforms is getting to be a real turn off. I got stopped by Stinky Gresham in the corridor yesterday. I weren't doing nothin' but she was like, 'Stand up straight, Carl.' And I was like 'Chill, Miss'. And she was like, 'Take your hand out of your pockets', which is no problem only then she starts going on about me tie. Like how it was knotted wrong. What's going on? Where is it writ in the school rules that there's a right way and a wrong way to knot your tie. I wasn't breaking no rules. My point is – if it's in the rules, fair enough. Only don't make up new rules on the spot.
>
> From
> Carl Smith

Score / 10

You will see that these questions require you to write for very different audiences. Continue on a separate sheet of paper if necessary.

You will be assessed for your writing skills, including the presentation of your work. Take special care with handwriting, spelling and punctuation.

Think about the purpose, audience and, where appropriate, the format of your writing.

1 You have been asked by your school council to write to your head teacher complaining about the amount of litter and graffiti in the school and making suggestions about how to deal with it. **(20 marks)**

Write your letter

The quality of your writing is more important than its length. You should write approximately one or two pages.

and

2 A magazine that you read is having a competition for young people who want to be journalists. The brief is to write a lively and interesting article, aimed at young people, about the most exciting day of your life. **(20 marks)**

Write your article

The quality of your writing is more important than its length. You should write approximately one or two pages.

Score   / 40

How well did you do?

| 0–19 | Try again | 20–29 | Getting there | 30–40 | Good work | 41–55 | Excellent! |

For more information on this topic, see pages 22–23 of your Success Revision Guide.

Writing to Argue

Multiple-choice questions

Choose just one answer: A, B, C or D.

1 Why might you use rhetorical questions when writing to argue? **(1 mark)**
- **A** To let your audience know that you are undecided.
- **B** To involve the audience.
- **C** To bring your argument to a conclusion.
- **D** To confuse your audience.

2 Why might you use repetition? **(1 mark)**
- **A** To reinforce an important point.
- **B** To amuse the audience.
- **C** To present irrelevant information.
- **D** To disguise your lack of arguments.

3 When arguing a case, you should: **(1 mark)**
- **A** ignore the other side of the argument
- **B** give equal weight to both sides
- **C** take into account the opposite view but explain why you think it is wrong
- **D** give the opposite view without commenting on it.

4 Your opening paragraph should be: **(1 mark)**
- **A** long
- **B** understated
- **C** powerful and clear
- **D** complicated and indecisive.

5 Your final paragraph should: **(1 mark)**
- **A** ask the readers to decide
- **B** introduce a new argument
- **C** include an anecdote
- **D** reiterate your main points.

Score / 5

Short-answer questions

Which of the following are examples of writing to argue? Give yourself one mark for each correct answer.

(5 marks)

a) A letter to a newspaper giving your views on budget cuts.

b) A speech to the school parliament saying why you are against compulsory PE.

c) The answer to a letter to a magazine asking for help getting rid of your spots.

d) An article in the school magazine about the school concert.

e) A blog in which you try to convince your readers that Angelina Jolie is a better actress than Cameron Diaz.

f) A letter to the local council about the need for more bin collections.

g) An account of your holiday in Florida.

h) An entry in your diary.

i) A recipe for apple crumble.

j) A leading article in a newspaper, which gives the arguments for and against a war before coming down on one side or the other.

The correct answers to the question above could also be seen as 'writing to persuade', as you would probably want to persuade your readers to agree with your point of view.

Score / 5

These two questions both focus on writing to argue but have different target audiences and different formats. Continue on a separate sheet of paper.

1 Imagine that you are a member of a group that campaigns against experiments on animals. Write the text for a leaflet in which you **argue** that all experiments on animals are wrong and should be banned.

Think about purpose, audience and the format for your writing. You will also be assessed on your spelling, punctuation and presentation.

The quality of your writing is more important than its length. You should write about one or two pages.

and (20 marks)

2 You are a medical researcher working in a centre where experiments are sometimes performed on live animals. Write a letter to your local newspaper **arguing** the case for such experiments to remain legal.

Think about purpose, audience and the format for your writing. You will also be assessed on your spelling, punctuation and presentation.

The quality of your writing is more important than its length. You should write approximately one or two pages. (20 marks)

Non-Fiction

Score   / 40

How well did you do?

| 0–17 | Try again | 18–27 | Getting there | 28–37 | Good work | 38–50 | Excellent! |

For more information on this topic, see pages 24–25 of your Success Revision Guide.

Writing to Persuade

Multiple-choice questions

Choose just one answer: A, B, C or D.

How would the following features help to persuade readers to your point of view?

1 Facts and statistics. **(1 mark)**
  A By showing that you are cleverer than them.
  B By making them question your motives.
  C By providing evidence to back up your points.
  D By making them laugh.

2 Emotive language. **(1 mark)**
  A By upsetting them.
  B By making them feel sorry for you.
  C By making them feel empathy for someone else.
  D By inspiring appropriate emotions in them.

3 Personal pronouns such as 'you' and 'we'. **(1 mark)**
  A By involving them and making the argument seem relevant to them.
  B By making them feel guilty and wrong.
  C By inviting them to reply.
  D By showing them what a lovely person you are.

4 Conditional sentences. **(1 mark)**
  A By making them think about what would happen if they agree (or if they do not agree).
  B By showing them that you might be wrong after all.
  C By showing them that what you are writing about is not important.
  D By making them angry.

5 Discursive markers (or cohesive devices). **(1 mark)**
  A By making your argument 'flow' in a logical manner.
  B By demonstrating how many connectives you know.
  C By dividing up the page neatly.
  D By making your text look as if it was written by an adult.

Score / 5

Short-answer questions

Match the following 'sentence starters' with the appropriate sentences. Give yourself one mark for each correct answer. **(5 marks)**

1 In my experience...

2 Imagine what would happen if...

3 Do we really want a world where...

4 Many people believe...

5 What would the consequences be...

a) ...that one day half the population will be over a hundred years old.

b) ...if we all followed his advice and stopped eating meat?

c) ...all the nuclear reactors in the country shut down at once.

d) ...the truth is rarely pure and never simple.

e) ...elderly people are afraid to set foot outside their own homes?

Score / 5

These two questions both focus on writing to persuade but have different target audiences and different formats. Continue on a separate sheet of paper.

1 You are going to make a speech to your school assembly to try to **persuade** your audience to volunteer to help older people in your community. **(20 marks)**

Write your speech, including in it:

- who these people are and where they live
- the sorts of problems that they might have
- how we can help them
- why we should help them.

and

2 You have organised an event in your school to raise money for a local charity. You have been given the job of **persuading** a celebrity to attend the event. **(20 marks)**

Think about:

- what sort of event you have organised
- what you are going to do with the money you raise
- who the celebrity is
- why he or she might be interested in the event and the charity
- what difference a celebrity visit will make to the success of your event.

Write your letter.

Score   / 40

How well did you do?

| 0–17 | Try again | 18–27 | Getting there | 28–37 | Good work | 38–50 | Excellent! |

For more information on this topic, see pages 26–27 of your Success Revision Guide.

Non-Fiction

Writing to Inform and Explain

Multiple-choice questions

Choose just one answer: A, B, C or D.

1 What is the difference between writing to inform and writing to explain? **(1 mark)**
  A Informative writing is more entertaining than explanatory writing.
  B Informative writing uses more presentational devices.
  C Explanatory writing explains how and why things are as they are, whereas informative writing may only tell us about what they are.
  D One is factual and the other is not.

2 In what tense is explanatory writing usually written? **(1 mark)**
  A The past tense.
  B The present tense.
  C The future tense.
  D The future perfect tense.

3 What sort of tone should you usually aim for when writing to inform or explain? **(1 mark)**
  A Clear and balanced.
  B Emotive and passionate.
  C Amusing and eccentric.
  D Hectoring and sarcastic.

4 Which of the following punctuation marks is used to introduce a list? **(1 mark)**
  A A comma.
  B A semi colon.
  C A colon.
  D A full stop.

5 Which of the following should **not** be included in informative writing? **(1 mark)**
  A Bullet points.
  B Explanations of unfamiliar words.
  C Experts' views.
  D Lies.

Score   / 5

Short-answer questions

Match the following 'sentence starters' with the appropriate sentences. Give yourself one mark for each correct answer. **(5 marks)**

1 Although…

a) …why I think that it is important for all you to have this injection.

2 Let me explain…

b) …only a relatively small proportion of cancers prove fatal.

3 Many people want to know how…

c) …they can avoid paying too much tax without breaking the law.

4 Contrary to popular belief…

d) …thing to remember is to fill the pool with water before jumping in.

5 The most important…

e) …you will come across many different makes of dishwasher, they all work in basically the same way.

Score   / 5

These two questions both focus on writing to inform and explain but have different target audiences and different formats. Continue on a separate sheet of paper.

1 Write a letter to a pen friend who lives abroad, informing them about a hobby or interest that you enjoy and **explaining** why you enjoy it. Assume that your friend knows nothing at all about your hobby. (20 marks)

and

2 Write an entry for your school website **informing** parents about forthcoming events at the school.

You should include: (20 marks)

- what the events are
- who is involved in them
- when they will be taking place
- where they will taking place
- why they are important.

Score / 40

How well did you do?

| 0–17 | Try again | 18–27 | Getting there | 28–37 | Good work | 38–50 | Excellent! |

For more information on this topic, see pages 28–29 of your Success Revision Guide.

Narrative Writing and Genre

Multiple-choice questions

Choose just one answer: A, B, C or D.

1 What is the main purpose of creative writing? **(1 mark)**
- **A** To inform and explain.
- **B** To persuade your readers to agree with your point of view.
- **C** To entertain and engage your readers.
- **D** To educate your readers.

2 What is the 'plot' of a story? **(1 mark)**
- **A** An important theme in the story.
- **B** The events of the story.
- **C** The way in which the story is told.
- **D** The end of the story.

3 What is meant by a 'genre'? **(1 mark)**
- **A** A type or category of text.
- **B** The language you write in.
- **C** The purpose of your writing.
- **D** The length of your text.

4 In which genre would you expect to find dark imagery, an ominous atmosphere and supernatural events? **(1 mark)**
- **A** Horror
- **B** Romance
- **C** Adventure
- **D** Science Fiction

5 In which genre would you expect to find magic, mythical creatures and heroism? **(1 mark)**
- **A** Mystery
- **B** Fantasy
- **C** Satire
- **D** Chick Lit

Score   / 5

Short-answer questions

Most stories can be divided into four parts.

1 Put the four parts in the correct order: (4 marks)

a) Resolution   **b)** Exposition   **c)** Complication   **d)** Climax

2 Now match them with following explanations: (4 marks)

a) The point of the story when the tension reaches its highest point.

b) The part of the story where characters and settings are established.

c) The part in which a problem or issue, which changes the course of the plot, is introduced.

d) The part where the tension is relaxed and problems are things are sorted out.

a) ....   b) ....   c) ....   d) ....

3 What do you think is meant by the 'inciting incident' in a story? (2 marks)

....

....

Score   / 10

GCSE-style questions

Continue on a separate sheet of paper if necessary.

You will be assessed on both your ability to produce an interesting, organised and appropriate piece of writing and the use of varied sentence structures and correct spelling, grammar and punctuation.

1 Narrative writing. (20 marks)

Write an account of a frightening experience.

....

....

....

....

....

....

....

and

2 Descriptive writing. (20 marks)

Describe, in both summer and winter, **either**

a) a shopping centre, **or**

b) a fairground, **or**

c) a beach

....

....

....

....

....

....

....

....

Score   / 40

How well did you do?

| 0–19 | Try again | 20–29 | Getting there | 30–40 | Good work | 41–55 | Excellent! |

For more information on this topic, see pages 34–35 of your Success Revision Guide.

Characterisation and Imagery

Multiple-choice questions

Choose just one answer: A, B, C or D.

1 A narrative that uses the pronoun 'I' is known as: **(1 mark)**
  A a first-person narrative
  B a second-person narrative
  C a third-person narrative
  D an impersonal narrative.

2 A third-person narrator who can see into all the characters' minds is known as: **(1 mark)**
  A an omnipotent narrator
  B an omnipresent narrator
  C an omniscient narrator
  D a know-all.

3 Which of the following is an example of alliteration? **(1 mark)**
  A The car door clanged shut.
  B Great green goats go gently.
  C Big elephants can always use small elephants.
  D Cool fools down tools.

4 Which of the following sentences includes onomatopoeia? **(1 mark)**
  A The fireworks fizzed and crackled through the still darkness.
  B The sound it made reminded me of childhood holidays.
  C It was a magnificent explosion of colour.
  D Her voice was music to my ears.

5 What is a cliché? **(1 mark)**
  A A word that does not make sense.
  B A foreign word or phrase imported into English.
  C An example of bad grammar.
  D An overused phrase.

Score   / 5

Short-answer questions

1 What sort of weather might you describe if you were using personification to convey your character's joy or optimism? .... **(2 marks)**

2 What is the difference between a metaphor and a simile? **(2 marks)**

3 Which of the following is a metaphor and which is a simile? **(2 marks)**

  a) Callum was as jittery as a bag of angry toads. ....

  b) He might be my cousin but I can't stand the little toad. ....

4 The following sentences use common symbols: what do they usually represent? **(4 marks)**

  a) Last Christmas I gave you my **heart**. ....

  b) Behold the **lamb** of God. ....

  c) Climb every **mountain**. ....

  d) Beyond the village lay a dark **forest**. ....

Score   / 10

Some examination boards test creative or imaginative writing in an exam, while others test it through controlled assessment. On this page, page 31 and page 33, you will find a variety of questions in different styles to choose from.

Continue on a separate sheet of paper if necessary.

This task contains two parts.

1 Write an article for a magazine in which you describe a place that means a lot to you. **(10 marks)**

and

2 **either**

a) write a letter from someone who lives in the place, responding to your article. **(10 marks)**

or

b) write a review of the place for a website, giving views that contrast with those in your article. **(10 marks)**

or

c) write the text for a leaflet about one of the main tourist attractions in the place. **(10 marks)**

Score / 20

Creative Writing

How well did you do?

| 0–13 | Try again | 14–20 | Getting there | 21–27 | Good work | 28–35 | Excellent! |

For more information on this topic, see pages 36–37 of your Success Revision Guide.

Transforming Texts

Multiple-choice questions

Choose just one answer: A, B, C or D.

1 What is meant by 're-creative writing'? **(1 mark)**
- **A** Writing that is especially creative.
- **B** Writing about sports and hobbies.
- **C** Writing that copies someone else's original work exactly.
- **D** Writing that is based on an original text but adapts and transforms it.

2 Why would you use a thesaurus to help your creative writing? **(1 mark)**
- **A** It gives you the meanings of words.
- **B** It gives words that are different but mean exactly the same thing.
- **C** It gives words with similar or related meanings to use as alternatives.
- **D** It gives you longer words, which will impress your readers.

3 Why might you occasionally use a very short paragraph in your creative writing? **(1 mark)**
- **A** To create impact and emphasis.
- **B** To explain something difficult.
- **C** To show that something is of little importance.
- **D** To build up a sense of mystery using description.

4 Why might you use ellipses (...)? **(1 mark)**
- **A** To create tension and make the reader wonder what might happen next.
- **B** To end a long paragraph.
- **C** To indicate that something is funny.
- **D** To show the reader that you have not finished your story.

5 What is persona? **(1 mark)**
- **A** A female person.
- **B** Any character in a play or film.
- **C** The person to whom a poem is addressed.
- **D** A fictional identity taken on by the writer.

Score / 5

Short-answer questions

1 The following are well-known examples of 're-creative writing', having been inspired by other texts. Find out which text each was based on. Give yourself one mark for each correct answer. **(5 marks)**

a) *10 Things I Hate About You* ....

b) *West Side Story* ....

c) *The Wide Sargasso Sea* ....

d) *Clueless* ....

e) *Return to The Forbidden Planet* ....

2 Explain briefly what is meant by re-creative writing. **(2 marks)**

....

....

Score / 7

Continue on a separate sheet if necessary.

1 Write a monologue or a series of diary entries, using the voice of a character from a text that you have studied (it could be a play, a novel, a short story or a poem). You should invent a new story for the character, rather than describing what happens in the original text. **(10 marks)**

and

2 either

a) Write an obituary for a newspaper, reflecting on your chosen character's life. **(10 marks)**

or

b) Write a letter to a newspaper from a different character in the same text defending his or her actions. **(10 marks)**

or

c) Write two or three poems describing the feelings of another character at key moments in the original text. **(10 marks)**

Score   / 20

How well did you do?

| 0–11 | Try again | 12–18 | Getting there | 19–25 | Good work | 26–32 | Excellent! |

For more information on this topic, see pages 38–39 of your Success Revision Guide.

Studying Shakespeare

Multiple-choice questions

Choose just one answer: A, B, C or D.

1 What is meant by 'the fatal flaw' in Shakespearean tragedy? **(1 mark)**
- **A** An illogical development in the plot.
- **B** An aspect of the tragic hero's character that will lead to his downfall.
- **C** An aspect of the tragic hero's character that will mean he is successful.
- **D** A crime somebody commits that leads to death.

2 Shakespeare's history plays: **(1 mark)**
- **A** are 100% accurate
- **B** are completely fictional
- **C** were the Elizabethan equivalent of 'Horrible Histories'
- **D** were based on sources that may not always have been accurate.

3 Shakespeare's comedies: **(1 mark)**
- **A** are based on true stories
- **B** are written entirely in prose
- **C** end happily for most of the characters
- **D** end sadly for most of the characters.

4 What does 'pastoral' mean in literature? **(1 mark)**
- **A** A rather idealised version of rural life.
- **B** A play where all the characters are very caring.
- **C** A brutally realistic version of rural life.
- **D** A play or poem about priests or vicars.

5 Which of the following statements is **not** true? **(1 mark)**
- **A** Shakespeare wrote during the Elizabethan and Jacobean periods.
- **B** Most of Shakespeare's plays were originally performed in daylight.
- **C** Originally female parts in Shakespeare's plays were played by boys or young men.
- **D** Shakespeare's plays were very unpopular when they were first performed.

Score / 5

Short-answer questions

Shakespeare's plays are often divided into tragedies, comedies and histories.

Put the following plays into the correct columns:

a) *Romeo and Juliet*

b) *Hamlet*

c) *As You Like It*

d) *Henry V*

e) *Richard III*

f) *Macbeth*

g) *Othello*

h) *Twelfth Night*

i) *Henry IV, Part One*

j) *A Midsummer Night's Dream*

Tragedies	Comedies	Histories

Score / 10

Some examination boards test your understanding of Shakespeare in an exam, while others test it through controlled assessment. On the following pages you will find a variety of questions in different styles to choose from. Choose those that most closely resemble the style of the exam or controlled assessment you will be sitting.

The following two questions are controlled assessment questions, in which Shakespeare texts are linked to poetry. If this is the kind of task you expect to be taking but you have not studied either of the plays mentioned, substitute the title of the Shakespeare play you have studied.

Continue on a separate sheet of paper if necessary.

Either

1 **a)** How does Shakespeare present attitudes to love in *Twelfth Night*? **(20 marks)**

b) Compare the different attitudes shown to love in two or three of the poems you have studied.

c) What is your response to the presentation of the theme of love in *Twelfth Night* and in the poetry you have studied?

or

2 **a)** Consider how Shakespeare presents war and conflict in *Henry V*. **(20 marks)**

b) Compare how two or three different poets present conflict.

c) Give your personal response to the ways in which conflict is presented in the literature you have been studying.

Score / 20

Shakespeare

How well did you do?

0–13 Try again   14–20 Getting there   21–27 Good work   28–35 Excellent!

For more information on this topic, see pages 42–43 of your Success Revision Guide.

Shakespeare's Use of Language

Multiple-choice questions

Choose just one answer: A, B, C or D.

1 What is the correct term for the metre in which most of Shakespeare's work is written? **(1 mark)**
- **A** Iambic hexameter.
- **B** Trochaic pentameter.
- **C** Iambic pentameter.
- **D** Trochaic hexameter.

2 How many stressed syllables would a line written in that metre contain? **(1 mark)**
- **A** Five.　**B** Four.　**C** Six.　**D** None.

3 When would Shakespeare typically use a rhyming couplet? **(1 mark)**
- **A** At the end of a scene or to emphasise key thoughts.
- **B** At the beginning of a scene or to show deep emotion.
- **C** Throughout a comedy.
- **D** Never.

4 Which of the following is an example of an oxymoron? **(1 mark)**
- **A** Have not saints lips?
- **B** She does teach the torches to shine bright.
- **C** O heavy lightness!
- **D** A preserving sweet.

5 Which of the following statements is correct? **(1 mark)**
- **A** Shakespeare's plays were written in a mixture of prose and verse.
- **B** Some of Shakespeare's plays were written in verse and some in prose.
- **C** Shakespeare's plays were written entirely in verse.
- **D** Shakespeare wrote his plays in prose but somebody else turned them into verse.

Score　/ 5

Short-answer questions

Read the extract from *Macbeth*. Macbeth has just killed King Duncan. Answer on a separate sheet.

Enter Macbeth
MACBETH　I have done the deed. – Didst thou not hear a noise?
LADY MACBETH　I heard the owl scream and the crickets cry.
　　Did not you speak?
MACBETH　When?
LADY MACBETH　Now.
MACBETH　As I descended?
LADY MACBETH　Ay.
MACBETH　Hark! – Who lies i' the second chamber?
LADY MACBETH　Donalbain.
MACBETH　This is a sorry sight　　[*looking at his hands*]
LADY MACBETH　A foolish thought to say a sorry sight.
MACBETH　There's one did laugh in's sleep, and one cried 'Murder!'
　　That they did wake each other: I stood and heard them:
　　But they did say their prayers, and address'd again to sleep.
LADY MACBETH　There are two lodg'd together.
MACBETH　One cried 'God bless us' and 'Amen' the other;
　　As they had seen me with these hangman's hands.
　　Listening their fear I could not say 'Amen'
　　When they did say 'God bless us.'

1 How would you describe the state of mind of Macbeth in this extract? **(2 marks)**

2 How would you describe Lady Macbeth's state of mind? **(2 marks)**

3 How would you describe the mood and atmosphere of the scene? **(2 marks)**

4 How does Shakespeare use language to increase tension? **(2 marks)**

5 Why is Macbeth so concerned about not being able to say 'Amen'? **(2 marks)**

Score　/ 10

GCSE-style questions

Continue on a separate sheet if necessary.

Answer both parts **a)** and **b)**.

a) How does Shakespeare present Lady Macbeth's thoughts and feelings in the extract below? **(10 marks)**

and

b) Write about Lady Macbeth's thoughts and feelings in a different part of the play. **(10 marks)**

> **LADY MACBETH** That which hath made them drunk hath made me bold.
> What hath quenched them hath given me fire. Hark! Peace!
> It was the owl that shrieked, the fatal bellman,
> Which gives the stern'st good night. He is about it;
> The doors are open: and the surfeited grooms
> Do mock their charge with snores: I have drugged their possets,
> That death and nature do contend about them
> Whether they live or die.
> **MACBETH** *(within)* Who's there? What, ho
> **LADY MACBETH** Alack! I am afraid they have awak'd
> And tis not done: – the attempt and not the deed
> Confounds us. – Hark! – I laid their daggers ready;
> He could not miss 'em. – Had he not resembled
> My father as he slept, I had done't. – My husband!

Score   / 20

How well did you do?

| 0–13 | Try again | 14–20 | Getting there | 21–27 | Good work | 28–35 | Excellent! |

For more information on this topic, see pages 44–45 of your Success Revision Guide.

Romeo and Juliet

Shakespeare

Multiple-choice questions

Choose just one answer: A, B, C or D.

1 Which of the following characters is a Capulet? **(1 mark)**
- **A** Friar Lawrence
- **B** Romeo
- **C** Juliet
- **D** Balthazar

2 Which of the following is a Montague? **(1 mark)**
- **A** Romeo
- **B** Juliet
- **C** Tybalt
- **D** The nurse

3 Which of the following does Capulet want Juliet to marry? **(1 mark)**
- **A** Tybalt
- **B** Mercutio
- **C** Romeo
- **D** Paris

4 In which city is the play set? **(1 mark)**
- **A** Verona
- **B** Venice
- **C** Vienna
- **D** Rome

5 What is a feud? **(1 mark)**
- **A** An ongoing quarrel or dispute between families.
- **B** A huge feast given by a family.
- **C** A murder committed by a family member.
- **D** A sporting competition between families.

Score / 5

Short-answer questions

Here are some of the main events of *Romeo and Juliet*. Try to put them in the correct order. (10 marks)

a) Romeo kills Tybalt and is banished to Mantua.

b) There is a fight between the Montagues and Capulets in the streets of Verona.

c) Romeo and Juliet kill themselves.

d) Romeo and Juliet get married.

e) Mercutio, Benvolio and Romeo go to the Capulets' feast.

f) Tybalt kills Mercutio.

g) Romeo and Juliet meet for the first time.

h) Juliet takes a potion and, appearing to be dead, is taken to the Capulets' vault.

i) Romeo climbs over the orchard wall and Juliet appears on the balcony.

j) Capulet tells Juliet to marry Paris.

1	2	3	4	5
6	7	8	9	10

Score / 10

GCSE-style questions

Continue on a separate piece of paper if necessary.

If your exam board sets questions in this style but you have not studied *Romeo and Juliet,* try rewriting the questions, substituting the title of the play you have studied.

Either

1 Write about the female characters in *Romeo and Juliet.* How does their presentation reflect the time when the play was written? **(20 marks)**

or

2 Discuss the presentation of conflict and violence in *Romeo and Juliet.* How do the attitudes shown in the play reflect the time when it was written? **(20 marks)**

or

3 Write about how religious beliefs are shown in *Romeo and Juliet.* How do the attitudes shown reflect the time when the play was written? **(20 marks)**

Score   / 20

How well did you do?

| 0–13 | Try again | 14–20 | Getting there | 21–27 | Good work | 28–35 | Excellent! |

For more information on this topic, see pages 46–47 of your Success Revision Guide.

Writing an Essay on *Romeo and Juliet*

Multiple-choice questions

Choose just one answer: A, B, C or D.

1 At what time of day is Act 3, Scene 5 of *Romeo and Juliet* set? **(1 mark)**
 A Dawn
 B Noon
 C Evening
 D Midnight

2 What important event took place on the previous day? **(1 mark)**
 A Romeo and Juliet met for the first time.
 B Romeo married Rosaline.
 C Romeo and Juliet were married.
 D Paris and Juliet were married.

3 Why does Romeo have to go to Mantua? **(1 mark)**
 A He has been given a job to do there.
 B He has been exiled from Verona after killing Tybalt.

 C He has been exiled for killing Mercutio.
 D He needs a holiday.

4 Why does Juliet feel betrayed by the nurse? **(1 mark)**
 A The nurse has told her mother about Romeo.
 B The nurse tells her to forget Romeo and marry Paris.
 C The nurse says she will tell the Prince that Romeo is still in Verona.
 D The nurse says she is going to leave the Capulets.

5 What does Juliet say she will do if Friar Lawrence cannot help her? **(1 mark)**
 A Kill herself.
 B Kill Romeo.
 C Run away to Mantua.
 D Marry Paris.

Score   / 5

Short-answer questions

Below are two speeches from Act 3, Scene 5 of *Romeo and Juliet:* one is from the very beginning of the scene and the other from the end. Continue on a separate sheet of paper if necessary.

1 Describe the change in Juliet's mood and attitude that has taken place during the scene. (3 marks)

....

....

> Wilt thou be gone? It is not yet near day.
> It was the nightingale and not the lark
> That pierced the fearful hollow of thine ear.
> Nightly she sings on yond pomegranate tree.
> Believe me, love, it was the nightingale

2 Explain why this change had taken place. (3 marks)

....

....

> Ancient damnation! O most wicked fiend,
> Is it more sin to wish me thus forsworn,
> Or to dispraise my lord with the same tongue
> Which she hath praised him with above compare
> So many thousand times? Go, counsellor.
> Thou and my bosom henceforth shall be twain.
> I'll to the Friar to know his remedy.
> If all else fail, myself have power to die.

3 Analyse how this change is reflected in her language. (4 marks)

....

....

Score   / 10

Answers

For GCSE-style questions marked out of 10, marks are approximately equivalent to the following grades:

9–10	A*
8	A
7	B
6	C
5	D
4	E
3	F
2	G
0–1	U

For GCSE-style questions marked out of 20, marks are approximately equivalent to the following grades:

18–20	A*
16–17	A
14–15	B
12–13	C
10–11	D
8–9	E
6–7	F
4–5	G
0–3	U

Back to Basics (pages 4–5)

Multiple-choice questions
1 C
2 B
3 A
4 D
5 D

Short-answer questions
1 Last Monday, Kelly and Ruksana were overjoyed when they heard Justin Bieber was in town. Unfortunately, neither of them was able to get tickets for the concert. Just after lunch, while Kelly was at dance practice, Ruksana received a text from her friend, Elle. It said that Justin had just arrived at his hotel and Elle was outside. Not only had she seen him, she had taken a picture of him getting out of his car!

2 'Can you come out tonight?' asked Tom. 'We're going for a pizza.'
'I'm not sure,' Jon replied. 'Mum wants me to go to Nan's. It's her sixtieth birthday.'
'That sounds like fun.'
'Yeah, plus she wants me to do the shopping. I've got a massive list: cake, jellies, sausage rolls, chicken drumsticks and just about everything else.'

GCSE-style questions
Use the following mark scheme as a guide.
1–4 marks
- Punctuation (full stops, commas, capital letters to start sentences) is attempted and often used correctly.
5–7 marks
- Commas, full stops, capital letters, question marks and punctuation for direct speech are used, usually correctly.
8–10 marks
- A range of punctuation is used deliberately and correctly, perhaps including colons, semi-colons, brackets and dashes.

Writing Skills (pages 6–7)

Multiple-choice questions
1 C
2 A
3 B
4 B
5 C

Short-answer questions
Possible answers:
1 a) I stayed off school yesterday **because** I had a stomach ache.

b) She might have gone to the supermarket, **but** she could still be at work.
c) **Although** my grandmother is over eighty, she still enjoys aerobics.
d) The dog was scratching at the door, **so** we let him out.
e) We were really enjoying the programme **until** the dog spoilt it by barking at the television.

2 Possible answer:
I left work early that day because I had a headache. While I was waiting at the bus stop, a woman, who was very tall with red hair, stopped to talk to me. She told me that she came from Darlington, which surprised me because it is long way off. She said that she had taken the wrong bus, and now she had to get home. However, she was at the wrong bus stop. Having told her where to go, I offered to take her, but she said she would be all right. Nevertheless, she walked off in the wrong direction.
I shouted to her, but she did not turn round. As she turned the corner, I ran after her. She had disappeared.

GCSE-style questions
Use the following mark scheme as a guide.
1–4 marks
- Punctuation (full stops, commas, capital letters to start sentences) is attempted and often used correctly.
- Sentences are mostly simple or compound (using conjunctions such as 'and', 'but' and 'so').
- There might be some attempt to use paragraphs.
5–7 marks
- Commas, full stops, capital letters, question marks and punctuation for direct speech are used, usually correctly.
- Sentences are varied, including both complex and compound sentences.
- Paragraphs are used to create a sense of order and organisation.
8–10 marks
- A range of punctuation is used deliberately and correctly, perhaps including colons, semi-colons, brackets and dashes.
- A variety of simple, compound and complex sentences is used to create effects.
- Paragraphs are used to structure the writing and are effectively connected.

Writing Skills (pages 8–9)

Multiple-choice questions
1 C
2 B
3 A
4 D
5 D

Short-answer questions
Last **Wednesday** I was supposed to be travelling to Spain to see my grandmother. **However**, while I was packing, I **heard** on the radio that there was very bad **weather** over France, as a result of **which** all flights were subject to delay or even **cancellation**. I **panicked**. I just didn't know what to do – **whether** to go to the airport and hope for the best, or stay at home and try to rearrange my trip. I **knew** my grandmother would be very **disappointed** if I didn't get **there**.

GCSE-style questions
Use the following mark scheme as a guide.
1–4 marks
- Punctuation (full stops, commas, capital letters to start sentences) is attempted, often correctly.
- Sentences are mostly simple or compound (using conjunctions such as 'and', 'but' and 'so').
- There might be some attempt to use paragraphs.
- Spelling of simple words is accurate but there are errors with more unusual or complex words.
5–7 marks
- Commas, full stops, capital letters, question marks and punctuation for direct speech are used, usually correctly.
- Sentences are varied, including both complex and compound sentences.
- Paragraphs are use to create a sense of order and organisation.
- Spelling of simple words is correct. More unusual or complex words are usually spelt correctly.

8–10 marks
- A range of punctuation is used deliberately and correctly, perhaps including colons, semi-colons, brackets and dashes.
- A variety of simple, compound and complex sentences is used to create effects.
- Paragraphs are used to structure the writing and are effectively connected.
- Spelling is almost always correct.

Reading Non-Fiction (pages 10–11)

Multiple-choice questions
1 C
2 A
3 D
4 B
5 A

Short-answer questions
1 To explain and inform
2 To inform and persuade
3 To explain and inform
4 To entertain, inform, explain and advise
5 To entertain, describe, inform and review.

GCSE-style questions
Use the following mark scheme as a guide.
1 **1 mark** for each fact (Italy's largest lake; formed by glaciation; Sirmione has a population of 5,100).
2 **1 mark** for each persuasive word (e.g. tranquil, luxurious, dramatic, glorious, seduced, picturesque), and up to **2 marks** for each convincing explanation of the word's effect (e.g. 'tranquil' would appeal to people who have busy lives and want a quiet and peaceful holiday'); 'dramatic' suggests that a visit to Garda might be exciting and adventurous; 'seduced' makes the reader think about the place as if it were a person to fall in love with.

Conventions and Features (pages 12–13)

Multiple-choice questions
1 B
2 D
3 A
4 C
5 B

Short-answer questions
1 Presentational features: bullet points; logo; subheading; illustration; bold font.
   Linguistic features: hyperbole; imperative; oxymoron; metaphor; assonance. (Up to **5 marks**)
2 • Hyperbole
   • Rule of three (used twice)
   • Rhetorical question
   • Use of personal pronouns ('you', 'our' and 'us')
   • Imperative
   • Exclamation
   • Modal verb
   • Emotive language. (Up to **5 marks**)

GCSE-style questions
Use the following mark scheme as a guide.
1 **1 mark** for identifying some words from the text and repeating information.
   2–3 marks for identifying and commenting on several relevant words and phrases (e.g. 'steadfast for over 185 years'; 'last year alone...'; 'six out of ten of all lifeboat launches...').
   4–5 marks for detailed exploration of the text, and giving an overview of its use of language to inform.
2 **1 mark** for identifying some appropriate words and phrases.
   2–3 marks for identifying and commenting on several relevant words and phrases (e.g. 'courageous and selfless'; 'caring and responsible'; 'those in peril on the sea').
   4–5 marks for detailed exploration of the text, analysing the connotations of language used, and giving an overview of its use of language to persuade.

Writing Techniques (pages 14–15)

Multiple-choice questions
1 B
2 A
3 D
4 A
5 A

Short-answer questions
1 Fact – a statistic backed up by its source.
2 Opinion – indication of a personal belief in 'I am convinced', and emotive language.
3 Opinion – use of modal verb 'should' and strong language with no 'factual' back up.
4 Fact – statistics and facts presented without comment or any sense of judgement.
5 Opinion – quotation attributed to a particular person – view strongly expressed in simile.

GCSE-style questions
Use the following mark scheme as a guide.
1 **1 mark** for each fact up to a total of **5 marks**: he's eight; passed A level maths with a grade A; youngest person to score As in all modules; did not get 100%; passed first module when 7; attends primary school in Leicester; he is in a class of 30; sat papers over 3 days; his father is called Moussa and is 48.
2 Possible answer:
   A genius is someone who is extremely clever and the writer is telling us about Yasha's very unusual achievement. He stresses the boy's age and that he has achieved something that is very rare in much older people, in a subject many find difficult. He mentions that his background is quite ordinary, perhaps making us think that his ability comes naturally, making it the result of 'genius' rather than hard work. (Up to **5 marks**)

Audience (pages 16–17)

Multiple-choice questions
1 D
2 A
3 B
4 A
5 C

Short-answer questions
Tabloids: a, b, c, e, f, h, i, j, k, l, m, n
Broadsheets: a, d, f, g, i, j, k, l, m, n

GCSE-style questions
Use the following mark scheme as a guide.
- **1–2 marks** for an answer that just repeats what is said in the article, perhaps making some brief comments.
- **3–4 marks** for an answer that identifies important details of language (e.g. the pun 'sum'; use of the word genius) and presentation (e.g. headline; bold print).
- **5–6 marks** for an answer that covers the details above and makes relevant points about their impact on the reader.
- **7–8 marks** for an answer that discusses the article in detail, also giving an overview of the effect of the article, using appropriate terminology.
- **9–10 marks** for a thorough, detailed and convincing answer that shows a complete understanding of the use of both language and presentational features.

Writing Non-Fiction (pages 18–19)

Multiple-choice questions
1 A
2 C
3 B
4 D
5 D

Short-answer questions
1 a) To inform, explain and advise (or instruct)
   b) To inform and persuade
   c) To inform, entertain, review and describe
   d) To argue and persuade.
2 a) Fashion-conscious women
   b) Children (perhaps boys)

Answers

c) General adult audience (perhaps well educated)

d) Farmers.

GCSE-style questions

Use the following mark scheme as a guide.

Both questions require you write formal letters, using the correct format and polite, formal and persuasive English. Use the person's name and sign off with 'Yours sincerely'.

1–9 marks

- Basic awareness of purpose and audience
- Makes some relevant points
- May not always be in appropriate language
- Limited vocabulary
- Might be attempting to use paragraphs
- Simple and compound sentences
- Basic punctuation correct
- Simple words spelt correctly.

10–14 marks

- Awareness of purpose and audience
- Makes relevant points and supports them with evidence/detail
- Attempts to adapt style and language
- Beginning to vary vocabulary for effect
- Paragraphs used logically with topic sentences
- More varied sentences, including simple, compound and complex
- A range of punctuation usually correctly used
- Spelling of most words correct.

15–20 marks

- Clear understanding of purpose and audience
- Shows a sense of purpose, develops and supports points made
- Style and language appropriate to the task
- A wide range of vocabulary used precisely and to create effects
- Paragraphs used consciously and confidently to order writing
- A full range of sentence structures used
- A wide range of punctuation used correctly
- Spelling, including that of irregular words, is almost always correct.

Writing for Different Audiences (pages 20–21)

Multiple-choice questions

1 D
2 B
3 B
4 A
5 C

Short-answer questions

Possible answer:

> Dear Mr Banks,
>
> On behalf of the pupils, I would like to share our concern with some recent events in school. I particularly refer to the issue of school uniform, which is beginning to alienate many pupils. Yesterday, I was stopped by Miss Gresham in the corridor. Although I do not believe that I was doing anything wrong, she told me stand up straight and, when I asked her to calm down, to take my hands out of my pockets. I agree that she has every right to ask me to do this. However, she then told me that my tie was knotted incorrectly. I would like to know whether there is a rule about how a tie should be knotted. I do not believe there is. In which case, teachers should not be able to make up new rules whenever it suits them.
>
> Yours sincerely
>
> Carl Smith

(Up to **10 marks**)

GCSE-style questions

Use the following mark scheme as a guide.

Question 1 requires a formal, polite tone and should be set out correctly as a formal letter. Use the person's name and sign off with 'Yours sincerely'.

Question 2 requires you to write an article for people your own age, so it should be less formal, more friendly, and livelier in style. You should include a headline, sub-headings, a strapline and a by-line, as well as writing in short paragraphs.

1–19 marks

- Basic awareness of purpose and audience
- Makes some relevant points
- May not always be in appropriate language
- Limited vocabulary
- Might be attempting to use paragraphs
- Simple and compound sentences
- Basic punctuation correct
- Simple words spelt correctly.

20–29 marks

- Awareness of purpose and audience
- Makes relevant points and supports them with evidence/detail
- Attempts to adapt style and language
- Beginning to vary vocabulary for effect
- Paragraphs used logically with topic sentences
- More varied sentences, including simple, compound and complex
- A range of punctuation usually correctly used
- Spelling of most words correct.

30–40 marks

- Clear understanding of purpose and audience
- Shows a sense of purpose, develops and supports points made
- Style and language appropriate to the task
- A wide range of vocabulary used precisely and to create effects
- Paragraphs used consciously and confidently to order writing
- A full range of sentence structures used
- A wide range of punctuation used correctly
- Spelling, including that of irregular words, is almost always correct.

Writing to Argue (pages 22–23)

Multiple-choice questions

1 B
2 A
3 C
4 C
5 D

Short-answer questions

a), b), e), f), j)

GCSE-style questions

Use the following mark scheme as a guide.

The answer to question 1 should be argumentative and persuasive in tone, using fact-based evidence and emotive language. It should be written in paragraphs, using headlines, sub-headings and other presentational devices such as bullet points.

The answer to question 2 should be in the form of a letter, starting 'Dear Sir' and ending 'Yours faithfully'. Its tone should be argumentative and persuasive, with fact-based evidence but probably a more balanced feeling than the answer to question 1.

1–19 marks

- Basic awareness of purpose and audience
- Makes some relevant points
- May not always be in appropriate language
- Limited vocabulary
- Might be attempting to use paragraphs
- Simple and compound sentences
- Basic punctuation correct
- Simple words spelt correctly.

20–29 marks

- Awareness of purpose and audience
- Makes relevant points and supports them with evidence/detail
- Attempts to adapt style and language
- Beginning to vary vocabulary for effect
- Paragraphs used logically with topic sentences
- More varied sentences, including simple, compound and complex
- A range of punctuation usually correctly used
- Spelling of most words correct.

30–40 marks
- Clear understanding of purpose and audience
- Shows a sense of purpose, develops and supports points made
- Style and language appropriate to the task
- A wide range of vocabulary used precisely and to create effects
- Paragraphs used consciously and confidently to order writing
- A full range of sentence structures used
- A wide range of punctuation used correctly
- Spelling, including that of irregular words, is almost always correct.

Writing to Persuade (pages 24–25)

Multiple-choice questions

1 C
2 D
3 A
4 A
5 A

Short-answer questions

1 d)
2 c)
3 e)
4 a)
5 b)

GCSE-style questions

Use the following mark scheme as a guide.

Question 1 requires an informal, persuasive tone. You should include plenty of evidence, perhaps examples and anecdotes. You might want to use emotive language as well as other rhetorical devices, such as rhetorical questions and lists of three. You should make plenty of use of the pronouns 'we' and 'you' to involve your audience.

Question 2 asks for a letter. You should aim at being formal yet friendly, persuading your celebrity with flattery as well as facts, emotive stories, etc. Use the person's name and sign off with 'Yours sincerely'.

1–19 marks
- Basic awareness of purpose and audience
- Makes some relevant points
- May not always be in appropriate language
- Limited vocabulary
- Might be attempting to use paragraphs
- Simple and compound sentences
- Basic punctuation correct
- Simple words spelt correctly.

20–29 marks
- Awareness of purpose and audience
- Makes relevant points and supports them with evidence/detail
- Attempts to adapt style and language
- Beginning to vary vocabulary for effect
- Paragraphs used logically with topic sentences
- More varied sentences, including simple, compound and complex
- A range of punctuation usually correctly used
- Spelling of most words correct.

30–40 marks
- Clear understanding of purpose and audience
- Shows a sense of purpose, develops and supports points made
- Style and language appropriate to the task
- A wide range of vocabulary used precisely and to create effects
- Paragraphs used consciously and confidently to order writing
- A full range of sentence structures used
- A wide range of punctuation used correctly
- Spelling, including that of irregular words, is almost always correct.

Writing to Inform and Explain (pages 26–27)

Multiple-choice questions

1 C
2 B
3 A
4 C
5 D

Short-answer questions

1 e)
2 a)
3 c)
4 b)
5 d)

GCSE-style questions

Use the following mark scheme as a guide.
The answer to question 1 should be in the form of a friendly, informal letter. You know the recipient quite well but you should bear in mind that he or she may not understand the references or expressions that a British teenage might be familiar with. Use first names.
For the answer to question 2 write in a fairly informal style, but bear in mind that you have an audience of parents, so you need to adjust your language. It is also important that everything is very clearly expressed. Use paragraphs, headings and other appropriate presentational devices, such as bullet points (but not illustrations).

1–19 marks
- Basic awareness of purpose and audience
- Makes some relevant points
- May not always be in appropriate language
- Limited vocabulary
- Might be attempting to use paragraphs
- Simple and compound sentences
- Basic punctuation correct
- Simple words spelt correctly.

20–29 marks
- Awareness of purpose and audience
- Makes relevant points and supports them with evidence/detail
- Attempts to adapt style and language
- Beginning to vary vocabulary for effect
- Paragraphs used logically with topic sentences
- More varied sentences, including simple, compound and complex
- A range of punctuation usually correctly used
- Spelling of most words correct.

30–40 marks
- Clear understanding of purpose and audience
- Shows a sense of purpose, develops and supports points made
- Style and language appropriate to the task
- A wide range of vocabulary used precisely and to create effects
- Paragraphs used consciously and confidently to order writing
- A full range of sentence structures used
- A wide range of punctuation used correctly
- Spelling, including that of irregular words, is almost always correct.

Narrative Writing and Genre (pages 28–29)

Multiple-choice questions

1 C
2 B
3 A
4 A
5 B

Short-answer questions

1 b), c), d), a)
2 **a)** d) Climax
  b) b) Exposition
  c) c) Complication
  d) a) Resolution
3 An event that starts the story off.

GCSE-style questions

Use the following mark scheme as a guide.

1–19 marks
- Some awareness of purpose and audience
- Some focus on the task
- May not always be in appropriate language
- Limited vocabulary
- Might be attempting to use paragraphs
- Simple and compound sentences
- Basic punctuation correct, but not all the time
- Simple words spelt correctly.

20–29 marks
- Generally in control of the material
- Awareness of purpose and audience
- Fairly good focus on the task
- Attempts to adapt style and language to the task
- Beginning to vary vocabulary for effect
- Paragraphs used properly with a sense of direction
- More varied sentences, including simple, compound and complex
- A range of punctuation usually correctly used
- Spelling of most words correct.

30–40 marks
- Sophisticated control of the material
- Clear understanding of purpose and audience
- Very clear focus on the task
- Style and language appropriate to the task
- A wide range of vocabulary used precisely and to create effects
- Paragraphs (and perhaps other structural devices) used consciously and confidently to order writing
- A full range of sentence structures used
- A wide range of punctuation used correctly
- Spelling, including that of irregular words, is almost always correct.

Characterisation and Imagery (pages 30–31)

Multiple-choice questions
1 A
2 C
3 B
4 A
5 D

Short-answer questions
1 Bright and sunny.
2 A metaphor describes something or someone as if it is something else (an implied comparison), while a simile compares, using 'like' or 'as'.
3 a) simile
   b) metaphor
4 a) Love and romance.
   b) Innocence and sacrifice.
   c) A difficulty or an obstacle to be overcome, or an ambition
   d) The unknown.

GCSE-style questions
Use the following mark scheme as a guide.
1–9 marks
- Basic awareness of purpose and audience
- Makes some relevant points
- May not always be in appropriate language
- Limited vocabulary
- Might be attempting to use paragraphs
- Simple and compound sentences
- Basic punctuation correct
- Simple words spelt correctly.

10–14 marks
- Awareness of purpose and audience
- Makes relevant points and supports them with evidence/detail
- Attempts to adapt style and language
- Beginning to vary vocabulary for effect
- Paragraphs used logically with topic sentences
- More varied sentences, including simple, compound and complex
- A range of punctuation usually correctly used
- Spelling of most words correct.

15–20 marks
- Clear understanding of purpose and audience
- Shows a sense of purpose, develops and supports points made
- Style and language appropriate to the task
- A wide range of vocabulary used precisely and to create effects
- Paragraphs used consciously and confidently to order writing
- A full range of sentence structures used
- A wide range of punctuation used correctly
- Spelling, including that of irregular words, is almost always correct.

Transforming Texts (pages 32–33)

Multiple-choice questions
1 D
2 C
3 A
4 A
5 D

Short-answer questions
1 a) *The Taming of The Shrew*
   b) *Romeo and Juliet*
   c) *Jane Eyre*
   d) *Emma*
   e) *The Tempest*

2 Re-creative writing is original or creative writing that is inspired by or loosely based on another text.

GCSE-style questions
Use the following mark scheme as a guide.
1–19 marks
- Some awareness of purpose and audience
- Some focus on the task
- May not always be in appropriate language
- Limited vocabulary
- Might be attempting to use paragraphs
- Simple and compound sentences
- Basic punctuation correct, but not all the time
- Simple words spelt correctly.

20–29 marks
- Generally in control of the material
- Awareness of purpose and audience
- Fairly good focus on the task
- Attempts to adapt style and language to the task
- Beginning to vary vocabulary for effect
- Paragraphs used properly with a sense of direction
- More varied sentences, including simple, compound and complex
- A range of punctuation usually correctly used
- Spelling of most words correct.

30–40 marks
- Sophisticated control of the material
- Clear understanding of purpose and audience
- Very clear focus on the task
- Style and language appropriate to the task
- A wide range of vocabulary used precisely and to create effects
- Paragraphs (and perhaps other structural devices) used consciously and confidently to order writing
- A full range of sentence structures used
- A wide range of punctuation used correctly
- Spelling, including that of irregular words, is almost always correct.

Studying Shakespeare (pages 34–35)

Multiple-choice questions
1 B
2 D
3 C
4 A
5 D

Short-answer questions
Tragedies: a), b), f), g)
Comedies: c), h), j)
Histories: d), e), i)

GCSE-style questions
Use the following mark scheme as a guide.
1–7 marks
- Mostly re-telling the story
- Some general comments made
- Simple points of comparison
- Simple expression of preferences.

8–11 marks
- Some understanding of the main features of the text
- Some relevant detail selected
- Some comments about language, form and structure
- Some similarities and differences pointed out.

12–15 marks
- More detailed references to the text
- Characters and relationships discussed in some detail
- Understanding of ideas and themes
- Understanding of how language, form and structure create effects
- Exploration of links and comparisons in more detail.

16–20 marks
- Confident selection of relevant detail
- Original ideas
- Evaluation of characters and motivation
- Written persuasively and cogently
- Appreciation of how writers use form, structure and language to create effects
- Analysis of writers' techniques
- Sustained links and comparisons.

Points you may have included

1 *Twelfth Night*
   a) • For most of the play, most of the characters are in love with the wrong person.
      • Orsino's love for Olivia is 'poetic' and self-indulgent.
      • Malvolio's love for Olivia is seen as ridiculous because of his status as well as his character.
      • Sir Andrew is set up to court Olivia for material gain.
      • Olivia's love for Viola/Caesario is similar to Orsino's for her – both sad and comic because Viola is really a woman.
      • Viola's feelings for Orsino appear to be hopeless because she seems to be the wrong gender and the wrong status, but in fact her feelings are true and are eventually returned.
      • Toby and Maria's relationship is simple, based on lust and pleasure, but it also leads to cruelty.
      • Olivia's mourning for her brother is excessive.
      • Viola and Sebastian are so close they are almost one person.
      • During *Twelfth Night* all the 'rules' are broken, but in the end order is restored and everyone has an appropriate partner.
   b) Your answer will differ according to the poetry you have studied, but you should consider:
      • who is speaking and to whom
      • what sort of love is described
      • whether the love is returned
      • the form the poem takes (e.g. sonnet form, ballad form)
      • how the poem is organised
      • the use of rhythm and rhyme
      • the language used
      • the use of imagery
      • the poet's attitudes to and feelings about love.
   c) Focus on comparing the texts, considering both similarities and differences, and on giving your own personal response. Think about how they make you feel.

2 *Henry V*
   a) • The main conflict is the war between England and France.
      • From the start, Henry is seen as justified in going to war.
      • There has been a long history of conflict between the countries and Henry is seen as bringing it to an end.
      • Henry is seen as an inspirational leader and a model king.
      • Henry is held in high regard in spite of his past – as a young man he was immoral and in conflict with his father.
      • The effects of war on ordinary soldiers are shown, but the soldiers are still behind Henry.
      • There is a great sense of excitement about the battles.
      • There is also some conflict with opponents at home but, again, Henry is seen as being fair and just.
      • Henry's love for Katherine is presented comically as a sort of conflict.
      • In the end order is restored and peace established.
   b) Your answer will differ according to the poetry you have studied, but you should consider:
      • who is speaking and to whom
      • what sort of conflict is described, e.g. war, arguments between friends, politics
      • the causes and outcomes of the conflicts
      • the form the poem takes (e.g. sonnet form, ballad form)
      • how it is organised
      • use of rhythm and rhyme
      • language used
      • use of imagery
      • the poet's attitudes to and feelings about conflict and war.
   c) Focus on comparing the texts, considering both similarities and differences, and on giving your own personal response. Think about how the texts make you feel.

Shakespeare's Use of Language (pages 36–37)

Multiple-choice questions
1 C
2 A
3 A
4 C
5 A

Short-answer questions
Possible answers:
1 He is nervous and worried, feeling guilty after killing the King.
2 She is also feeling the tension but is calmer than her husband and does not really understand his feelings.
3 It is very tense and the atmosphere is quite eerie and perhaps frightening.
4 Macbeth and Lady Macbeth speak in short, even one-word, sentences, The dialogue seems 'chopped up' and they do not always answer each other.
5 He knows that he has committed a terrible sin and thinks that being unable to pray means that he has cut himself off from God and will be damned.

GCSE-style questions
Use the following mark scheme as a guide.

1–9 marks
• Some simple explanation of the extract and the play as a whole
• Some details used to support comments
• Awareness of the characters' feelings
• Awareness of the themes.

10–14 marks
• More sustained response, showing understanding of the extract and the play as a whole
• Points supported by detailed reference to the text
• Thoughtful comment on themes and ideas
• Appreciation of the effect of Shakespeare's language.

15–20 marks
• Insight shown into the extract and the whole play
• Detailed analysis of details from the text
• Evaluation of the effects of Shakespeare's language
• Convincing/imaginative interpretation of themes and ideas.

Points you may have included
a) • The extract takes place while Macbeth is killing Duncan.
   • Lady Macbeth waits nervously for his return.
   • She is worried that Macbeth might not kill the King.
   • She feels determined and bold.
   • Nevertheless, her reaction to the owl's shriek might suggest she is nervous.
   • The broken-up speech also indicates tension.
   • Her reaction to hearing Macbeth shows that she sees him as being weaker than she is.
   • Her reference to Duncan resembling her father might show a little bit of compassion or doubt, but it is easily overcome..
b) Scenes you might choose to write about include Act 1, Scene 5, where Lady Macbeth receives Macbeth's letter, and Act 5, Scene 1, the sleepwalking scene. You should think about how and why Lady Macbeth's character changes between the two scenes.

Romeo and Juliet (pages 38–39)

Multiple-choice questions
1 C
2 A
3 D
4 A
5 A

Short-answer questions
1 b)
2 e)
3 g)
4 i)
5 d)
6 f)
7 a)
8 j)
9 h)
10 c)

GCSE-style questions
Use the following mark scheme as a guide.

1–9 marks
• Simple comments made about characters and themes
• Quite brief and based on story-telling.

10–14 marks
• More focused answer with discussion of and empathy for characters
• Understanding of themes and language and structure.

15–20 marks
• Thoughtful answer, with close reference to the text
• Analysis of structure, form and language
• Insight into characters and themes.

Points you may have included

1 There are only three female characters: Juliet, Lady Capulet and the Nurse. You might also mention Rosaline, who is mentioned as a woman whom Romeo thinks he loves.

Juliet
- A girl from Juliet's class would be expected to obey her parents and marry a man of their choice.
- Her age is talked about. Most of the audience would probably think she was too young to marry, but it is said to be acceptable 'here in Verona'.
- Initially she comes across as a dutiful daughter.
- She defies conventions by disobeying her parents, but she will not 'break the rules' by sleeping with Romeo without being married.
- She depends on others to help her and, in the end, is powerless.

Lady Capulet
- Lady Capulet does as her husband asks.
- She cannot understand why Juliet would not marry Paris.
- Her relationship with her daughter is not very close.

Nurse
- The nurse has brought up Juliet.
- Although she is of low status she has more influence than Lady Capulet.
- She helps Juliet and seems to support her, but in the end she is pragmatic.
- Her lack of loyalty and morality shocks Juliet.

2
- The play is set in Italy, some time before it was written.
- Violent feuds between families were common in Italy.
- Family loyalty is seen as being of the utmost importance.
- Nobody seems to know why the two families are quarrelling, which shows the pointlessness of it all.
- Conflicts are resolved by violence.
- Violence and killing seem to come easily to the characters.
- There is an absolute ruler (the Prince) who uses the law to try to bring order.
- Friar Lawrence, as a representative of the Church, tries to end conflict.
- Love and violence are seen as two sides of the same coin.
- Violent acts lead to more violent acts.
- As well as conflict between families, there is conflict between generations.

3
- There are many references to religion and it is assumed that all the characters are Christian, at least in name.
- Friar Lawrence can be seen as representing the Church. He tries to end the feud and help Romeo and Juliet, and he is Romeo's confessor, advising him about right and wrong.
- Romeo and Juliet use a lot of religious imagery to describe their feelings. This could be read as meaning their love is holy and pure or it could mean that their love is blasphemous and they are putting each other before God.
- Romeo and Juliet are married by the Friar, making their union holy. Because of this it cannot be broken, so Juliet is bound to Romeo not just by love but also by duty.
- In the end they commit a terrible sin by killing themselves yet they do not seem to be condemned for it.

Writing an essay on *Romeo and Juliet* (pages 40–41)

Multiple-choice questions

1 A
2 C
3 B
4 B
5 A

Short-answer questions

Possible answers:

1 At the beginning Juliet is deeply in love. She is happy but conscious that Romeo has to leave. By the end of the scene she is angry and afraid, but determined.
2 Romeo has left for Mantua, and Juliet's parents (who do not know that she has secretly married Romeo) have told her that she must marry Paris. The nurse has told her to go along with this and forget Romeo, leaving her feeling betrayed.
3 The first speech is gentle and musical, with soft sounds and images taken from nature. In the second speech her language is harsh and accusing.

GCSE-style questions

Use the following mark scheme as a guide.

1–9 marks
- Beginning to make links between texts
- Reference made to aspects of form, structure and language
- Some understanding of the play and performed version
- Occasional reference to the text.

10–14 marks
- Some explanation of links and connections between texts
- Comment on the effects of language, form and structures
- Personal response to the play and performed version
- Points supported with appropriate detail.

15–20 marks
- A thorough explanation of connections between texts
- Perceptive and sensitive analysis of language, form and structure
- Insight into and engagement with the play and performed version
- Evaluation of relevant detail from the play and performed version.

Points you may have included
- This scene starts at dawn, after Romeo and Juliet have consummated their marriage.
- They are shown to be deeply in love.
- Juliet tries to persuade Romeo to stay. However, they are both aware of the danger he is in.
- The romantic imagery they use is sad as well as joyful – there are many references to death.
- It is as if they, like the audience, know how their story will end.
- The mood changes dramatically when Romeo has left.
- Juliet's reaction to the idea of marrying Paris shocks her parents.
- The violence of Capulet towards Juliet contrasts with his attitude earlier in the play.
- Juliet's parents believe she has a duty to obey them.
- Juliet cannot do as they ask because she is already married.
- The nurse's betrayal leaves Juliet feeling alone and desperate.
- Consider how the characters have changed since the start of the play – have they matured? have they discovered true love?
- Consider different ways of portraying the characters in versions you have seen – e.g. Juliet can be played as very frivolous and childish, or as innocent and more serious.

Writing an Essay on *Romeo and Juliet* (pages 42–43)

Multiple-choice questions

1 C
2 B
3 A
4 B
5 D

Short-answer questions

Possible answers:

1 Romeo does not want to leave Juliet and loves her so much that he will do whatever she wants, including dying.
2 Lady Capulet, not knowing about Juliet's love for Romeo, thinks that her daughter is upset because of Tybalt's death and vows revenge on his killer, Romeo.
3 Capulet is angry with Juliet for disobeying him. His mood is violent, in contrast with how he appeared earlier in the play.
4 Lady Capulet has refused to take Juliet's side. She is cold and unfeeling.
5 The nurse is pragmatic and thinks that it would be best if Juliet forgot Romeo and married Paris. She seems to have completely changed her mind about Romeo and has no idea of Juliet's feelings.

GCSE-style questions

Use the following mark scheme as a guide.

1–9 marks
- Some simple explanation of the extract and the play as a whole
- Some details used to avoid comments
- Awareness of the characters' feelings
- Awareness of the themes.

10–14 marks
- More sustained response, showing understanding of the extract and the play as a whole
- Points supported by detailed reference to the text
- Thoughtful comment on themes and ideas
- Appreciation of the effect of Shakespeare's language.

15–20 marks
- Insight shown into the extract and the whole play
- Detailed analysis of details from the text
- Evaluation of the effects of Shakespeare's language
- Convincing/imaginative interpretation of themes and ideas.

Points you may have included

a) • This scene starts at dawn, after Romeo and Juliet have consummated their marriage.
- They are shown to be deeply in love.
- Juliet tries to persuade Romeo to stay. However, they are both aware of the danger he is in.
- However, Romeo says he will pretend it is not daylight and stay.
- As elsewhere in the play, Shakespeare uses a lot of imagery about light and dark.
- The romantic imagery they use is sad as well as joyful – there are many references to death.
- 'Come death and welcome' is a chilling reminder to the audience of what will happen – we already know from the prologue that they are doomed to die
- It is as if they, like the audience, know how their story will end.
- In the last line, Juliet's tone is urgent and anxious.

b) Romeo and Juliet have very few scenes together in the play. You could write about Act 1, Scene 5, where they first meet; Act 2, Scene 2, the balcony scene; or the final scene, Act 5, Scene 3. You should think about the different stages of their relationship and how their changing feelings are shown in their language and actions.

Studying Drama (pages 44–45)

Multiple-choice questions
1 C
2 A
3 D
4 D
5 A

Short-answer questions
1 Willie works as a shoemaker and can barely read or write.
2 He works in the basement. Coming from below might be symbolic of his low status at the start of the play.
3 This might indicate that things are going to change for him and that by the end of the play he might have fulfilled his potential.
4 She is clearly an important customer, probably rich and used to telling people what to do. She has spotted Willie's talent.
5 This shows how Willie is used to being treated and how he does not expect anything good to happen.

GCSE-style questions
Use the following mark scheme as a guide.

1–9 marks
- Awareness of themes and ideas
- Mostly story-telling
- Some details used to support points made
- Awareness of playwright's use of language, form and structure.

10–14 marks
- More sustained or thoughtful response to the task
- Points supported by detailed reference to the play
- Appreciation of how the playwright's choice of language, form and structure affects the audience
- Thoughtful consideration of themes and ideas.

15–20 marks
- Insight shown in the exploration of the play
- Close analysis of the text supports interpretation
- Evaluation of the playwright's choice of form, structure and language and how it affects the audience
- Convincing and/or original interpretation of themes and ideas.

Points you may have included
1 • The extract comes at the end of Act 2, probably before an interval.
- Maggie and Willie are about to get married.
- It makes us laugh while also making us think about marriage and the characters' relationship.
- Maggie still seems to be the boss in the relationship, addressing Willie as 'lad'; Willie does as he's told.
- Although he does not express his feelings, as we might expect from someone in love, Willie does say that Maggie is 'growing on' him, indicating that there are some warm feelings towards her.
- Love is not mentioned at all.
- At this point, the lives of all the characters change.

- When Maggie and Willie leave Hobson's, their fortunes improve and Hobson's fortune declines.
- Willie will start to become the man Maggie thinks he really is.
- Maggie's ideas about marriage contrast with the romantic ideas of her younger sisters.
- The marriage seems to be a business arrangement.
- However, there is a gently humorous tone which suggests that Maggie and Willie have affection and respect for each other, which might be more lasting than conventional romance.

2 • In the course of the play, Willie changes dramatically.
- At the start he is timid and thought of as stupid.
- He emerges from the cellar, as if that is where he belongs.
- He is frightened of Mrs Hepworth and Hobson.
- Nevertheless, it is clear from the beginning that he is a skilled man.
- Maggie recognises Willie's ability, but she is the boss and he obeys her just as he obeyed Hobson.
- In Act 3, after the marriage, he begins to assert himself more. He is learning to read and write and to run a business, but he is still in awe of Maggie.
- In Act 4 he takes control, defying Maggie as well as Hobson.
- As he grows in stature and confidence, Maggie starts to respect him and their love grows.
- At the end of the play he has become the man he always had the potential to become.

Character and Audience (pages 46–47)

Multiple-choice questions
1 B
2 A
3 A
4 B
5 C

Short-answer questions
Possible answers:
1 He is a figure of authority / he knows a lot more than anyone else / he is angry with people he is talking to / he has a burning sense of justice and fairness.
2 Ordinary people or working-class people. People we do not know or would not normally notice. Anyone.
3 Possible revolution, or the First and Second World Wars.
4 Shocked, frightened, ashamed, angry.
5 Members of the audience might have any of the reactions of the characters in the play. They might be more likely to agree with the Inspector, with the benefit of hindsight. They might feel that they should do something to improve society.

GCSE-style questions
Use the following mark scheme as a guide.

1–9 marks
- Awareness of themes and ideas
- Mostly story-telling
- Some details used to support points made
- Awareness of playwright's use of language, form and structure.

10–14 marks
- More sustained or thoughtful response to the task
- Points supported by detailed reference to the play
- Appreciation of how the playwright's choice of language, form and structure affects the audience
- Thoughtful consideration of themes and ideas.

15–20 marks
- Insight shown in the exploration of the play
- Close analysis of the text supports interpretation
- Evaluation of the playwright's choice of form, structure and language and how it affects the audience
- Convincing and/or original interpretation of themes and ideas.

Points you may have included
1 a) • Consider the description of Mr Birling in the stage directions when he first enters.
- He is clearly the head of the family.
- He is confident and likes to dominate.
- His speech is quite bombastic, as he 'lays down the law'.
- He has no self doubt.
- He is proud of being a 'self-made man' and his origins are shown in his speech and attitudes.
- This is in contrast with his wife and children.

- His attitude to his family shows that he is a traditional father – he indulges them with money but does not listen to them.
- He is aggressive towards the Inspector and refuses to take responsibility for Eva Smith's death.
- Unlike the younger generation, he does not appear to change his attitudes.

b) • Eva Smith's death is used to make all the characters face up to the consequences of their actions.
- She could be one girl or many – she represents the ordinary person.
- Each family member came across her in a different context but they all treated her badly.
- This shows that moral decisions have to be made in every aspect of our lives.
- Both business and personal decisions can have dreadful consequences for others.
- By setting the play in the past, Priestley helps the audience to see how short-sighted the characters are – some of the things that have happened in history could be the result of their selfishness.
- The Inspector gives a voice to Priestley's socialist ideas – he speaks directly to the characters and the audience, warning them of the consequences of not taking responsibility for others.

2 *Kindertransport*

a) • By changing from Eva to Evelyn, the protagonist has tried to escape her past, but the events of the play show that such an escape is impossible.
- As members of the audience, we wonder why she is so keen to change her identity.
- Scenes from the past are played out on the same set, alternating with scenes from the present; in this way we see how important memories are.
- Eva/Evelyn makes choices about her identity. These choices are not seen as right or wrong, but the reappearance of her mother shows that she cannot deny her identity.
- Her past is also the story of the twentieth century.
- The 'kindertransport' was an episode in the history of the Second World War and the Holocaust.
- The consequences of history cannot be ignored, and we can also learn from history.

b) • The rat-catcher is a figure from German folklore, similar to the Pied Piper of Hamelin.
- He is both a familiar, comforting character, and a slightly sinister one.
- He represents Eva's childhood.
- He also represents her identity as a German.
- The actor playing the part also plays all the other minor parts.
- This means that he is always present, reminding us of Eva's childhood.
- He is the only male actor – does this say anything about men and women?

Analysing a Moving Image (pages 48–49)

Multiple-choice questions
1 C
2 C
3 A
4 C
5 D

Short-answer questions
1 Possible answers include: birdsong, dialogue; actors mumbling in the background; music played by people on set; the sound of cars passing; thunder; animal sounds; doors slamming, etc.
2 Possible answers include: the actors; personal props; costumes; the set; natural scenery; non-speaking extras.

GCSE-style questions
Use the following mark scheme as a guide.

1–9 marks
- Some awareness of purpose and audience
- Some focus on the task
- Some specialist terminology used correctly
- Might be attempting to use paragraphs or other structural devices
- Simple and compound sentences
- Basic punctuation correct, but not all the time
- Simple words spelt correctly.

10–14 marks
- Awareness of purpose and audience
- Good focus on the task
- Specialist film terminology used and spelt correctly most of the time
- Paragraphs and other structural devices used confidently

- More varied sentences, including simple, compound and complex
- A range of punctuation usually correctly used
- Spelling of most words correct.

15–20 marks
- Clear understanding of purpose and audience
- Very clear focus on the task
- Specialist film terminology used confidently and appropriately, and spelt correctly
- A wide range of vocabulary used precisely and to create effects
- Paragraphs and other structural devices used consciously and confidently to order writing
- A full range of sentence structures used
- A wide range of punctuation used correctly
- Spelling, including that of irregular words, is almost always correct.

Analysing a Moving Image (pages 50–51)

Multiple-choice questions
1 A
2 A
3 C
4 B
5 D

Short-answer questions
1 pans
2 hand-held
3 special effects
4 extreme close-up
5 aerial

GCSE-style questions
Use the following mark scheme as a guide.

1–9 marks
- Some awareness of purpose and audience
- Some focus on the task
- Some specialist terminology used correctly
- Might be attempting to use paragraphs or other structural devices
- Simple and compound sentences
- Basic punctuation correct, but not all the time
- Simple words spelt correctly.

10–14 marks
- Awareness of purpose and audience
- Good focus on the task
- Specialist film terminology used and spelt correctly most of the time
- Paragraphs and other structural devices used confidently
- More varied sentences, including simple, compound and complex
- A range of punctuation usually correctly used
- Spelling of most words correct.

15–20 marks
- Clear understanding of purpose and audience
- Very clear focus on the task
- Specialist film terminology used confidently and appropriately, and spelt correctly
- A wide range of vocabulary used precisely and to create effects
- Paragraphs and other structural devices used consciously and confidently to order writing
- A full range of sentence structures used
- A wide range of punctuation used correctly
- Spelling, including that of irregular words, is almost always correct.

Novels and Short Stories (pages 52–53)

Multiple-choice questions
1 D
2 B
3 A
4 B
5 A

Short-answer questions
1 a) Charlotte Brontë
   b) George Eliot
   c) William Makepeace Thackeray
   d) Jane Austen
   e) George Orwell
2 An ending of a chapter or episode that leaves the reader or audience wondering what will happen next.
3 The main character or the person whose story is being told.

GCSE-style questions

Use the following mark scheme as a guide.

1–9 marks

- Awareness of themes and ideas
- Mostly story-telling
- Some details used to support points made
- Awareness of writer's use of language, form and structure.

10–14 marks

- More sustained or thoughtful response to the task
- Points supported by detailed reference to the text
- Appreciation of how the writer's choice of language, form and structure affects the reader
- Thoughtful consideration of themes and ideas.

15–20 marks

- Insight shown in the exploration of the text
- Close analysis of the text supports interpretation
- Evaluation of the writer's choice of form, structure and language and how it affects the reader
- Convincing and/or original interpretation of themes and ideas.

Points you may have included

1 *Pride and Prejudice*

Charlotte Lucas:

- Charlotte provides a contrast with her friend, Elizabeth.
- She is plain and not especially witty.
- She is realistic about her prospects in life.
- She makes a sensible marriage to Mr Collins after he is rejected by Elizabeth.
- Marriage for her is a matter of security and love does not seem to matter.
- After her marriage she is neither happy nor unhappy.
- She portrayed sympathetically, but other characters might feel sorry for her.

Mr Bennet:

- Mr Bennet is shown as a loving but not very assertive father.
- His relationship with Elizabeth is especially close.
- He does not seem especially interested in the rest of the family.
- He is witty and ironic but can seem a little cruel.
- He is drawn with affection but also with irony.

Mrs Bennet:

- Mrs Bennet is more of a figure of fun.
- She is overbearing and interferes in her daughters' lives.
- However, she is motivated by genuine concern for their future.
- She constantly misjudges people and can be embarrassing.
- Her marriage is not an ideal one.

Mr Collins:

- Mr Collins is one of several men who can be compared with Darcy.
- He proposes to Elizabeth but his motives are not clear.
- After being rejected, he turns his attentions to Charlotte; it would seem that he just wants a wife.
- He is very snobbish and in awe of Lady Catherine de Burgh.
- Many of the other characters laugh at him.
- He betrays his own character by what he says.

2 *The Withered Arm and Other Wessex Tales*

a) • Marriage is of much greater importance to women than it is to men.
- Sophy first considers marrying Sam because, she says, 'it would be a home for me.'
- When she marries Mr Twycott she respects rather than loves him.
- As a working-class woman her options are to be a maid or a seamstress.
- Once married, she spends her time doing her hair and trying to live up to the idea of being a 'lady'.
- She is defined in relation to her son and husband.
- As a widow, although she has a home, she has no real role.
- She feels she cannot re-marry without her son's permission and denies herself happiness.
- Consider how much of Sophy's unhappiness is due to her being a woman in a world where men hold power, and how much is because of her class.

b) You could use any of the other stories in the collection. Remember to discuss both similarities and differences between Sophy and the other characters. Consider whether their gender always limit women and contributes to tragedy, or whether some of them lead independent and fulfilled lives.

3 *Great Expectations*

The opening chapter is an obvious choice, or you might write about Pip's meeting with Miss Havisham, or the novel's ending. There are many other parts of the novel you could use – choose an episode that you know well and that had an impact on you.

- Dickens creates a mystery from the start with the appearance of Magwitch.
- His vivid descriptions of landscapes create an eerie atmosphere.
- He keeps information from us as we follow Pip's progress.
- He uses the first-person narrative to involve us in the story – we empathise with Pip and want to know how things turn out for him.
- Pip makes a lot of mistakes as he grows up – he often takes 'wrong turnings'.
- Both the marshes and London are, in their different ways, full of danger.
- The Victorian period is a time of great contrasts between rich and poor, especially in London, and Pip's 'great expectations' could easily come to nothing.

Literary Techniques (pages 54–55)

Multiple-choice questions

1 A
2 D
3 B
4 A
5 A

Short-answer questions

Possible answers:

1 It is a rural setting; in the country; perhaps on a farm.
2 They seem to be hard-working but quite happy.
3 Non-standard English, with a regional accent – like people from the south west of England.
4 It seems quite light-hearted or gossipy.
5 Probably the 'he' who has just married, and his new bride.

GCSE-style questions

Use the following mark scheme as a guide.

1–9 marks

- Awareness of themes and ideas
- Mostly story-telling
- Some details used to support points made
- Awareness of writer's use of language, form and structure.

10–14 marks

- More sustained or thoughtful response to the task
- Points supported by detailed reference to the text
- Appreciation of how the writer's choice of language, form and structure affects the reader
- Thoughtful consideration of themes and ideas.

15–20 marks

- Insight shown in the exploration of the text
- Close analysis of the text supports interpretation
- Evaluation of the writer's choice of form, structure and language and how it affects the reader
- Convincing and/or original interpretation of themes and ideas.

Points you may have included

1 • Dickens starts with an exclamation: 'Oh!' He writes as if he is chatting to us and wants to share gossip.
- He refers to Scrooge as an 'old sinner'.
- He uses lists of adjectives to build up a lively, detailed picture.
- He compares him, using similes, to hard flint and an oyster.
- He describes his 'coldness' as having a physical effect on him – it is reflected in his face, his movement and his voice. He seems to belong to the winter – 'a frosty rime was on his head'.
- The description of his meanness reaches its climax with a reference to Christmas, and the rest of the story will be about how Scrooge finds the spirit of Christmas.

2 a) • Dickens shows us all sections of society and how they act at Christmas, but he is especially concerned with the poor.
- Scrooge is shown refusing to give to charity.
- His attitude reflects that of many people now and then – the poor are not his concern.
- He does not pay his clerk well – Bob finds it difficult to look after his big family, but Scrooge is indifferent.
- The Ghost of Christmas Present shows Scrooge how other people live. He reveals the poor conditions people live in, but also shows him that people in poverty have the spirit of Christmas. He shows him the reality of the Cratchits' life and what their poverty will mean for Tiny Tim.
- Want and Ignorance are an awful warning of what poverty can lead to.
- Through the change in Scrooge, Dickens shows us that we can and should do something about poverty.

b) • Each 'stave' (chapter) focuses on a different ghost: each has a role in changing Scrooge.
- Marley appears to show him how he will end up if he carries on as he is; when he was alive, Marley was just like Scrooge.
- The Ghost of Christmas Past reminds Scrooge that he was not always like he is now.
- The sight of the lonely child causes sympathy.
- Scrooge is upset by the past but perhaps he is feeling sorry for himself.
- The Ghost of Christmas Present shows Scrooge how others live.
- He educates Scrooge about the lives of the poor and also shows him how much more joyful other people's lives are.
- By watching his nephew and the Cratchits, Scrooge begins to realise that money is not as important as love.
- The Ghost of Christmas Yet To Come gives Scrooge a terrible warning of how he might die alone, not missed by anyone, and with his possessions stolen by others.
- Between them, the spirits help Scrooge to discover the spirit of Christmas and to understand what it really means.

Exploring Culture in Prose (pages 56–57)

Multiple-choice questions
1 D
2 D
3 A
4 D
5 C

Short-answer questions
Possible answers:
1 The town seems to have seen better days. It is described as 'a tired old town'. Perhaps it was once a wealthy place, but it is now quite poor. The writer refers to both 'rainy weather' and 'sweltering shade'.
2 The weather goes from one extreme to another. It can be very rainy or extremely hot.
3 The writer uses the phrase 'when I first knew it', indicating that she is looking back. She mentions mules pulling carts and men in 'stiff collars'.
4 They dress formally, probably for work. Possibly their stiff collars reflects their manners too.
5 They do not appear to work, doing very little all day except trying to stay cool. They are compared to 'soft tea-cakes' wilting in the sun.

GCSE-style questions
Use the following mark scheme as a guide.
1–9 marks
- Awareness of themes and ideas
- Mostly story-telling
- Some details used to support points made
- Awareness of writer's use of language, form and structure.

10–14 marks
- More sustained or thoughtful response to the task
- Points supported by detailed reference to the text
- Appreciation of how the writer's choice of language, form and structure affects the audience
- Thoughtful consideration of themes and ideas.

15–20 marks
- Insight shown in the exploration of the text
- Close analysis of the text supports interpretation
- Evaluation of the writer's choice of form, structure and language and how it affects the audience
- Convincing and/or original interpretation of themes and ideas.

Points you may have included
1 • Scout and Jem are visiting the church with their maid, Calpurnia. They are the only white people there.
- We experience the church and the lives of the black people through the eyes of the first-person narrator.
- She recalls her reactions as a child.
- The first paragraph emphasises how separate the lives of black and white people are.
- We are reminded of the history of slavery.
- The fact that the white men use the church for gambling may show contempt for the people who built it. This is not explained: perhaps the church needs money and the white men pay for its use.
- The cemetery is nothing like what Scout, and probably the reader, would expect from a cemetery – even the smell is different.
- Although Scout and Jem are children, adults act respectfully towards them.

- Everything seems quite harmonious until Lula arrives. Lula creates tension, causing a reaction from Calpurnia.
- There is a feeling that the tension might be caused by Calpurnia bringing white children to the church.
2 • Calpurnia is Atticus's maid but, because he is widowed, she is much more important in the children's lives.
- Her position in the household shows the difference in status between black and white. However, Atticus treats her with respect, showing his character and principles.
- The children learn their manners and morals from Calpurnia, who introduces them to the black community.
- When Aunt Alexandra visits, Scout sees how most people treat black servants ('Don't talk like that in front of them').
- However well she is thought of by the family, she is still a servant, and the races remain separate in Maycomb.

Culture in *Of Mice and Men* (pages 58–59)

Multiple-choice questions
1 B
2 B
3 A
4 B
5 D

Short-answer questions
Possible answers:
1 Lennie seems anxious, trying hard to remember something but failing. Remembering the rabbits might show that he is fond of animals and that he is childish in nature.
2 George takes command of Lennie but is also protective. He is keen to get work.
3 Curley is unfriendly towards the other men. 'Calculating' could show that he was thinking in terms of what they could do for him, perhaps how he could make money. 'Pugnacious' tells us that he is aggressive, perhaps even violent.
4 She is attractive and knows it. Perhaps she is being deliberately provocative, as she would not be expected to be fully made-up on the ranch. The 'brittle' quality of her voice might indicate a vulnerability in her character.
5 Crooks is isolated from the other men. He is aware that the others do not want to mix with him because he is black and this makes him protective of his own privacy and rather defensive.

GCSE-style questions
Use the following mark scheme as a guide.
1–9 marks
- Awareness of themes and ideas
- Mostly story-telling
- Some details used to support points made
- Awareness of writer's use of language, form and structure.

10–14 marks
- More sustained or thoughtful response to the task
- Points supported by detailed reference to the text
- Appreciation of how the writer's choice of language, form and structure affects the audience
- Thoughtful consideration of themes and ideas.

15–20 marks
- Insight shown in the exploration of the text
- Close analysis of the text supports interpretation
- Evaluation of the writer's choice of form, structure and language and how it affects the audience
- Convincing and/or original interpretation of themes and ideas.

Points you may have included
1 • At the beginning there is a contrast between Curley's aggression and Lennie's passive attitude.
- Readers are likely already to be sympathetic towards Lennie.
- Lennie's weakness and child-like nature are emphasised as he looks 'helplessly' to George.
- George's response, encouraging Lennie to violence, might be surprising.
- Short sentences help to increase the tension.
- Most of the language is straightforward, with little description.
- The diction is violent and dialogue, colloquial and sometimes crude, is used effectively.
- The sudden change in Lennie as he attacks Curley is both shocking and thrilling.
- The simile 'like a fish on a line' effectively conveys the reversal in fortunes and Curley's weakness.

- The ending is frantic and frightening – George changes his attitude as he sees what is happening, but Lennie does not seem to realise what he has done.
- The passage gives us a powerful sense of what Lennie is capable of doing.
2 • George and Lennie are on the road, like many others, looking for work.
- They have to go anywhere and take any work they can.
- All the characters dream of a better life but they are all struggling to survive; life is hard and brutal on the ranch.
- Steinbeck presents a diverse group of people who have their own particular problems.
- Crooks lives apart from the other men because of his race.
- Curley's wife has no real identity and lives off hopeless dreams.
- Lennie could not survive on his own.
- In the end, George and Lennie's dream of a new life is shattered.
- The novel ends with a feeling of hopelessness and defeat.

Poetic Form and Features (pages 60–61)

Multiple-choice questions
1 A
2 D
3 B
4 A
5 A

Short-answer questions
1 a)
2 b)
3 c)
4 b)
5 a)
6 a)
7 b)
8 a)
9 c)
10 c)

GCSE-style questions
Use the following mark scheme as a guide.
1–9 marks
- Some response to the poems
- Some reference to the text
- Basic understanding of some features of language, form and structure.

10–14 marks
- Sustained response to the poems
- Well-chosen references to the text
- Clear understanding of some of the effects of language, form and structure.

15–20 marks
- Engagement with and insight into the poems
- Evaluation of and detailed reference to the text
- Insight into and evaluation of poets' use of language, form and structure.

Points you may have included
- Lucy lived an isolated life in the country.
- Very few people knew her or appreciated her beauty.
- She died as unknown as she lived.
- Her death has made a great difference to the poet.
- It is not clear what her relationship to the poet is and whether or not his feelings are romantic.
- The form is very simple: three stanzas of equal length; a regular rhyme scheme (*abab*); regular metre (iambic with four stresses on the first and third lines and three on the second and fourth).
- The poem follows a traditional ballad form – a ballad usually tells a story about ordinary people's lives. Together with the simplicity of the language, this makes it like a traditional, country song, suitable for the subject (a simple, country girl).
- The controlled and almost upbeat form might seem at odds with the subject matter when we realise that Lucy is dead.
- Lucy is compared in metaphor ('a violet') and simile ('fair as a star') to aspects of nature – she belongs to nature.
- The poet's feeling might not just be about Lucy but about all those whose lives pass unnoticed; he might be making a point about life and death in general.

Poetry Comparison (pages 62–63)

Multiple-choice questions
1 C
2 A
3 D
4 A
5 C

Short-answer questions
Possible answers:
1 The power, violence and beauty of nature.
2 In the first stanza an eagle stands on a rock. In the second it spots its prey and attacks.
3 It is referred to as 'he'. His natural surroundings are described like a fortress, as if he were a king. The eagle's talons are referred to as 'hands'.
4 The sounds are harsh, reflecting the bird's nature.
5 A thunderbolt is powerful and sudden; it is nature at its most violent. It might also remind us of mythological gods, such as Zeus or Thor.

GCSE-style questions
Use the following mark scheme as a guide.
1–9 marks
- Some response to the poems
- Some reference to the text
- Basic understanding of some features of language, form and structure.

10–14 marks
- Sustained response to the poems
- Well-chosen references to the text
- Clear understanding of some of the effects of language, form and structure.

15–20 marks
- Engagement with and insight into the poems
- Evaluation of and detailed reference to the text
- Insight into and evaluation of poets' use of language, form and structure.

When comparing poems, remember to comment on both similarities and differences. Among the areas you might compare are:
- the poem's subject matter
- the story of the poem (if any)
- the main themes and ideas
- the speaker
- the person addressed, if any
- form and structure
- rhyme
- metre/rhythm
- diction (choice of language)
- language techniques, such as alliteration, assonance, and onomatopoeia
- imagery, including similes and metaphors
- the poet's feelings and attitudes
- your response to the poems.

Presenting Information and Ideas (pages 64–65)

Multiple-choice questions
1 C
2 B
3 B
4 D
5 C

Short-answer questions
1 c), a), b), e), d)
2 a), e), b), d), c)

GCSE-style questions
Use the following mark scheme as a guide
1–9 marks
- Gives straightforward information and ideas
- Begins to adapt non-verbal features to audience and situation
- Uses varied vocabulary and structures, including some features of standard English.

10–14 marks
- Effectively communicates information and views
- Adapts talk and non-verbal features to situation and audience
- Uses varied vocabulary and sentence structures for effect
- Competent in use of standard English.

15–20 marks
- Tackles demanding subject matter, giving details and identifying priorities
- Uses a wide variety of verbal and non-verbal strategies
- Shows an assured and confident use of standard English vocabulary and grammar when appropriate.

Group Discussion and Drama (pages 66–67)

Multiple-choice questions
1 B
2 D
3 A
4 C
5 C

Short-answer questions
1 b)
2 c)
3 b)
4 a)
5 c)
6 a)
7 a)
8 b)
9 c)
10 b)

GCSE-style questions
Use the following mark schemes as a guide.

Group Discussion

1–19 marks
* Responds positively to others, asking for further detail, etc.
* Makes a few relevant contributions to discussion
* Allows others to express differing views.

20–29 marks
* Listens attentively, responding perceptively
* Makes significant contributions, moving the discussion on
* Engages with the ideas of others, recognising bias and referring to detail.

30–40 marks
* Shows understanding of complex ideas through questioning and response
* Shapes the discussion, responding with flexibility and challenging assumptions
* Encourages the participation of others, resolving differences and achieving useful outcomes.

Drama-based Activities

1–9 marks
* Shows some understanding of characters, creating straightforward roles
* Shows some understanding of issues and relationships.

10–14 marks
* Develops and sustains roles and characters
* Uses appropriate language and effective movement and gesture
* Shows understanding of and insight into issues and relationships.

15–20 marks
* Creates and sustains complex characters
* Uses a variety of dramatic techniques
* Explores and responds to complex ideas and issues.

Studying Spoken Language (pages 68–69)

Multiple-choice questions
1 B
2 C
3 D
4 A
5 D

Short-answer questions
Possible answers:
1 I was really keen on nursing, so I did my work experience in a hospital.
2 In my opinion the police do not know anything about gangs.
3 He told me that I had got it all wrong, but I did not understand what he meant.
4 There is no mountain high enough, not any river deep enough, to keep me from you.
5 No, I would be afraid to go into those fine places.

GCSE-style questions
Use the following mark scheme as a guide.

1–9 marks
* Some awareness of how spoken language is used for different purposes
* Understanding of some features of spoken language
* Awareness of attitudes to spoken language.

10–14 marks
* Confident explanation and some analysis of how language is used
* Explanation and analysis of features of spoken language

* Exploration and some analysis of attitudes to spoken language.

15–20 marks
* Perceptive analysis and evaluation of how spoken language is used
* Analysis and interpretation of features of spoken language
* Analysis and evaluation of attitudes to spoken language.

Studying Spoken Language (pages 70–71)

Multiple-choice questions
1 A
2 D
3 D
4 B
5 D

Short-answer questions
1 A short pause (also known as a 'micropause').
2 A pause lasting three seconds.
3 An overlap.
4 Elision.
5 A filler.

GCSE-style questions
Use the following mark schemes as a guide.

1–9 marks
* Some awareness of how spoken language is used for different purposes
* Understanding of some features of spoken language
* Awareness of attitudes to spoken language.

10–14 marks
* Confident explanation and some analysis of how language is used
* Explanation and analysis of features of spoken language
* Exploration and some analysis of attitudes to spoken language.

15–20 marks
* Perceptive analysis and evaluation of how spoken language is used
* Analysis and interpretation of features of spoken language
* Analysis and evaluation of attitudes to spoken language.

Mixed GCSE-Style Questions (pages 72–79)

In terms of GCSE grades, the marks you award for these questions are roughly equivalent to the following grades.
For questions marked out of 10:

9–10	A*
8	A
7	B
6	C
5	D
4	E
3	F
2	G
0–1	U

For questions marked out of 20:

18–20	A*
16–17	A
14–15	B
12–13	C
10–11	D
8–9	D
6–7	F
4–5	G
0–3	U

Reading Non-Fiction (page 72)
1 Award up to **5 marks**.
* 1 mark for a few simple points or unselective copying.
* 2–3 marks for a range of valid points backed up by reference to the text.
* 4–5 marks for selecting and explaining a range of valid points. The answer should be detailed and focused.

You could have made points such as:
* It is Italy's largest lake
* There are dramatic contrasts in scenery
* The lake and its surroundings are beautiful
* There are sandy beaches
* Poets and artists have been attracted to it
* It is ideal for activities such as walking and water sports
* It is very relaxing
* There are historical sites to visit

- There are many good restaurants
- There are very good hotels.

2 Award up to **5 marks**.
- 1 mark for identifying some appropriate words and phrases.
- 2–3 marks for identifying and commenting on several relevant words and phrases, e.g. 'a beautiful expanse'; 'glorious…scenery'; 'tranquil sandy shores'; and 'seduced by'.
- 4–5 marks for a detailed exploration of the text, analysing the connotations of language used, and giving an overview of the article's use of language to persuade.

3 Award up to **5 marks**.
- 1 mark for a few simple points or unselective copying.
- 2–3 marks for a range of valid points backed up by reference to the text.
- 4–5 marks for selecting and explaining a range of valid points. The answer should be detailed and focused.

You could have made points such as:
- The RNLI has been providing lifeboats for over 185 years.
- The sea is still very dangerous.
- Over 8,000 people were helped last year by the RNLI.
- Without donations the organisation would not exist.
- Six out of ten launches were made possible by money left in people's wills.
- If people leave money, the RNLI can carry on.

4 Award up to **5 marks**.
- 1 mark for identifying some people that the article might appeal to (e.g. 'old people').
- 2–3 marks for identifying and commenting on the identity of the desired audience, e.g. 'people who might be a little older and have money to leave' or 'those who are interested in the sea and care about others'.
- 4–5 marks for a detailed exploration of the text's intended audience, analysing the connotations of language used, and the possible identity of people who might be influenced by it, e.g. 'courageous and selfless' are emotive words that are designed to appeal to those who admire people who risk their lives for others. They might feel that leaving money to the RNLI would mean they too were selfless and would be helping the lifeboat crews, even though they themselves might not be brave enough to volunteer.

5 Award up to **10 marks**.
- 1 mark for a few simple points or unselective copying.
- 2–4 marks for simple comments based on the texts and showing awareness of meanings. At the lower end, answers might be rather confused; at the higher end, there will be some clear, if obvious, comparisons and contrasts.
- 5–7 marks for making valid comments and inferences based on detail from the texts. At the higher end, you will have shown that you can make detailed comparisons.
- 8–10 marks for making valid comments and inferences in a thorough and well-organised answer, selecting appropriate detail from the texts. The best answers will be coherent and confident.

6 Award up to **10 marks**.
- 1 mark for a few simple points or unselective copying.
- 2–4 marks for simple comments based on the texts and showing awareness of both writers' use of presentational devices, e.g. headlines and paragraphs.
- 5–7 marks for making valid comments and inferences based on several presentational devices. There will be a clear focus on presentational devices and their impact.
- 8–10 marks for making valid comments and inferences in a thorough and well-organised answer, selecting a wide range of presentational devices (including illustrations, sub-headings, fonts, colour, etc.) and analysing their use and effect on the reader.

Functional Writing (page 73)
Questions 1–6
Use the following mark scheme as a guide.
The questions require you to write with different purposes, to different audiences, and in different formats, and you should bear these in mind when applying the mark scheme, especially when considering the degree to which you have understood 'purpose and audience' and how appropriate your style and language are.
1–9 marks
- Basic awareness of purpose and audience
- Makes some relevant points
- May not always be in appropriate language
- Limited vocabulary

- Might be attempting to use paragraphs
- Simple and compound sentences
- Basic punctuation correct
- Simple words spelt correctly.
10–14 marks
- Awareness of purpose and audience
- Makes relevant points and supports them with evidence/detail
- Attempts to adapt style and language
- Beginning to vary vocabulary for effect
- Paragraphs used logically with topic sentences
- More varied sentences, including simple, compound and complex
- A range of punctuation usually correctly used
- Spelling of most words correct.
15–20 marks
- Clear understanding of purpose and audience
- Shows a sense of purpose, develops and supports points made
- Style and language appropriate to the task
- A wide range of vocabulary used precisely and to create effects
- Paragraphs used consciously and confidently to order writing
- A full range of sentence structures used
- A wide range of punctuation used correctly
- Spelling, including that of irregular words, is almost always correct.

Creative / Imaginative Writing (page 74)
Use the following mark scheme as a guide. Bear in mind that each of the tasks has a different purpose:
- **Narrative writing** is about telling a story well, structuring it effectively and retaining the reader's interest.
- **Descriptive writing** is about describing and creating atmosphere using the senses.
- **Personal writing** is reflective and concerned with your own life.
- **Re-creative writing** is inspired by an existing text and asks for an imaginative interpretation of it.
1–9 marks
- Basic awareness of purpose and audience
- Makes some relevant points
- May not always be in appropriate language
- Limited vocabulary
- Might be attempting to use paragraphs
- Simple and compound sentences
- Basic punctuation correct
- Simple words spelt correctly.
10–14 marks
- Awareness of purpose and audience
- Makes relevant points and supports them with evidence/detail
- Attempts to adapt style and language
- Beginning to vary vocabulary for effect
- Paragraphs used logically with topic sentences
- More varied sentences, including simple, compound and complex
- A range of punctuation usually correctly used
- Spelling of most words correct.
15–20 marks
- Clear understanding of purpose and audience
- Shows a sense of purpose, develops and supports points made
- Style and language appropriate to the task
- A wide range of vocabulary used precisely and to create effects
- Paragraphs used consciously and confidently to order writing
- A full range of sentence structures used
- A wide range of punctuation used correctly
- Spelling, including that of irregular words, is almost always correct.

Shakespeare (page 75)
1 *Twelfth Night*
Use the following mark scheme as a guide.
1–9 marks
- Some simple explanation of the extract and the play as a whole
- Some details used to avoid comments
- Awareness of the characters' feelings
- Awareness of the themes.
10–14 marks
- More sustained response, showing understanding of the extract and the play as a whole
- Points supported by detailed reference to the text
- Thoughtful comment on themes and ideas
- Appreciation of the effect of Shakespeare's language.
15–20 marks
- Insight shown into the extract and the whole play

- Detailed analysis of details from the text
- Evaluation of the effects of Shakespeare's language
- Convincing/imaginative interpretation of themes and ideas.

2 *Much Ado About Nothing*

Use the following mark scheme as a guide.

1–9 marks
- Simple comments made about characters and themes
- Quite brief and based on story-telling.

10–14 marks
- More focused answer with discussion of and empathy for characters
- Understanding of themes and language and structure.

15–20 marks
- Thoughtful answer, with close reference to the text
- Analysis of structure, form and language
- Insight into characters and themes.

Drama (page 76)
Questions 1–6

Use the following mark scheme as a guide.

1–9 marks
- Awareness of themes and ideas
- Mostly story-telling
- Some details used to support points made
- Awareness of playwright's use of language, form and structure.

10–14 marks
- More sustained or thoughtful response to the task
- Points supported by detailed reference to the play
- Appreciation of how the playwright's choice of language, form and structure affects the audience
- Thoughtful consideration of themes and ideas.

15–20 marks
- Insight shown in the exploration of the play
- Close analysis of the text supports interpretation
- Evaluation of the playwright's choice of form, structure and language and how it affects the audience
- Convincing and/or original interpretation of themes and ideas.

Prose (pages 77–78)
Questions 1–10

Use the following mark scheme as a guide.

1–9 marks
- Awareness of themes and ideas
- Mostly story-telling
- Some details used to support points made
- Awareness of writer's use of language, form and structure.

10–14 marks
- More sustained or thoughtful response to the task
- Points supported by detailed reference to the text
- Appreciation of how the writer's choice of language, form and structure affects the audience
- Thoughtful consideration of themes and ideas.

15–20 marks
- Insight shown in the exploration of the text
- Close analysis of the text supports interpretation
- Evaluation of the writer's choice of form, structure and language and how it affects the audience

Poetry: Writing about Unseen Poetry (page 79)

Use the following mark scheme as a guide.

1–9 marks
- Some response to the poems
- Some reference to the text
- Basic understanding of some features of language, form and structure.

10–14 marks
- Sustained response to the poems
- Well-chosen references to the text
- Clear understanding of some of the effects of language, form and structure.

15–20 marks
- Engagement with and insight into the poems
- Evaluation of and detailed reference to the text
- Insight into and evaluation of poets' use of language, form and structure.

Continue on a separate sheet of paper if necessary.

If your exam board sets questions in this style but you have not studied *Romeo and Juliet,* try rewriting the question, substituting a key scene and two major characters from the play you have studied.

Remind yourself of Act 3, Scene 5 in the text and one or two performed versions of the play that you have seen.

Using this scene as a starting point, and referring to the whole play, explore how the characters of Romeo and Juliet are portrayed in the performed versions you have studied.　　**(20 marks)**

You should consider:

• the thoughts and feelings Romeo and Juliet express

• the way other characters react to them

• the dramatic effect of the scene and its implications for the whole play.

Score　　/ 20

How well did you do?

0–13 | Try again　　14–20 | Getting there　　21–27 | Good work　　28–35 | Excellent!

For more information on this topic, see pages 48–49 of your Success Revision Guide.

Writing an Essay on *Romeo and Juliet*

Multiple-choice questions

Choose just one answer: A, B, C or D.

1 Which of these pairs of adjectives best describes the mood at the beginning of Act 3, scene 5? **(1 mark)**
- **A** Regretful and ashamed.
- **B** Angry and vengeful.
- **C** Tender and romantic.
- **D** Dark and brooding.

2 How might you describe Capulet's attitude to Juliet at the end of the scene? **(1 mark)**
- **A** Gentle and caring.
- **B** Authoritative and angry.
- **C** Cool and dispassionate.
- **D** Understanding and helpful.

3 Why would the nurse's suggestion that Juliet marries Paris be unacceptable in religious terms? **(1 mark)**
- **A** Juliet is already married to Romeo.
- **B** Juliet is too young to marry.
- **C** Paris is already married.
- **D** Paris is too old.

4 How many people (including themselves) know that Romeo and Juliet are married? **(1 mark)**
- **A** Three
- **B** Four
- **C** Five
- **D** Ten

5 How does Juliet feel at the end of the scene? **(1 mark)**
- **A** Happy and optimistic.
- **B** Indecisive.
- **C** Sad but resigned.
- **D** Fearful but determined.

Score / 5

Short-answer questions

Below are five quotations taken from Act 3, Scene 5 of *Romeo and Juliet*. Explain briefly what each one tells us about the speaker's feelings at that point in the scene. Answer on a separate sheet of paper.

1 ROMEO
Let me be ta'en, let me be put to death.
I am content, so thou wilt have it so (2 marks)

2 LADY CAPULET
We will have vengeance for it, fear thou not.
Then weep no more. (2 marks)

3 CAPULET
Hang thee young baggage, disobedient wretch!
I'll tell thee what – get thee to church a Thursday
Or never after look me in the face. (2 marks)

4 LADY CAPULET
Talk not to me, for I'll not speak a word.
Do as thou wilt, for I have done with thee. (2 marks)

5 NURSE
I think it best you married with the County.
O, he's a lovely gentleman.
Romeo's a dishclout to him. (2 marks)

Score / 10

GCSE-style questions

Continue on a separate sheet of paper if necessary.

Answer both parts **a)** and **b)**.

a) How does Shakespeare present the relationship between Romeo and Juliet in the extract below?   **(10 marks)**

and

b) Write about their relationship in a different part of the play.   **(10 marks)**

> **JULIET** Yond light is not daylight, I know it, I
> It is some meteor that the sun exhales
> To be to thee tonight a torch bearer
> And light thee on they way to Mantua.
> Therefore stay yet: thou need'st not be gone.
>
> **ROMEO** Let me be ta'en, let me be put to death.
> I am content, so thou wilt have it so.
> I'll say yon grey is not the morning's eye,
> 'Tis but the pale reflex of Cynthia's brow.
> Nor that is not the lark whose notes do beat
> The vaulty heaven so high above our heads.
> I have more care to stay than will to go.
> Come death and welcome. Juliet wills it so.
> How is't, my soul? Let's talk. It is not day.
>
> **JULIET** It is. It is. Hie hence, begone, away.

Score   / 20

How well did you do?

| 0–13 | Try again | 14–20 | Getting there | 21–27 | Good work | 28–35 | Excellent! |

For more information on this topic, see pages 50–51 of your Success Revision Guide.

Studying Drama

Multiple-choice questions

Choose just one answer: A, B, C or D.

1 A play is usually divided into: **(1 mark)**
  A chapters and paragraphs
  B stanzas
  C acts and scenes
  D columns.

2 Stage directions: **(1 mark)**
  A give information to the actors and director but are not spoken
  B give information to the audience and are spoken by a narrator
  C give alternative interpretations of the play
  D give the inner thoughts of the characters and are spoken aloud.

3 When writing about a play you should always consider the possible reactions of the: **(1 mark)**
  A readers   C examiners
  B customers   D audience.

4 A person who writes plays is known as: **(1 mark)**
  A a poet   C a playwriter
  B a novelist   D a playwright.

5 What is a soliloquy? **(1 mark)**
  A A speech made to the audience expressing the character's thoughts and feelings.
  B A speech made by a narrator telling the story.
  C A speech in which a character lies to the other characters.
  D Any long speech in a play.

Score   / 5

Short-answer questions

Read the following extract from *Hobson's Choice* by Harold Brighouse and, on a separate sheet of paper, answer the questions.

WILLIE MOSSOP comes up the trap. He is a lanky fellow, about thirty, not naturally stupid but stunted mentally by a brutalised childhood. He is a raw material of a charming man, but, at present, it requires a very keen eye to detect his potentialities. His clothes are a poorer edition of Tubby's. He comes half-way up trap.

MRS HEPWORTH Are you Mossop?
WILLIE Yes, mum.
MRS HEPWORTH You made these boots?
WILLIE (*peering at them*) Yes, I made them last week.
MRS HEPWORTH Take that.

WILLIE bending down, rather expects 'that' to be a blow. Then he raises his head and finds she is holding out a visiting card. He takes it.

MRS HEPWORTH See what's on it?
WILLIE (*bending over the card*) Writing?
MRS HEPWORTH Read it.
WILLIE I'm trying   (*His lips move as he tries to spell it out.*)

1 What do we learn about Willie's job and level of education? **(2 marks)**

2 Why do you think Willie makes his first entrance from below the stage? **(2 marks)**

3 What might the stage directions about Willie's 'potentialities' lead you to expect from the rest of the play? **(2 marks)**

4 What impression do you get of Mrs Hepworth? **(2 marks)**

5 What is the significance of Willie expecting Mrs Hepworth to hit him? **(2 marks)**

Score   / 10

Answer on a separate sheet of paper.

Here is an extract from *Hobson's Choice*.

MAGGIE	Well, Will, you've not had much to say for yourself today. How'st feeling, lad?
WILLIE	I'm going through with it, Maggie.
MAGGIE	Eh?
WILLIE	My mind's made up. I've got wrought up to a point. I'm ready.
MAGGIE	It's church we're going to, not the dentist's?
WILLIE	I know. You get rid of summat at dentist's, but it's taking summat on to go to church with a wench, and the Lord knows what.
MAGGIE	Sithee, Will, I've respect for a church. Yon's not the place for lies. The parson's going to ask you will you have me and you'll either answer truthfully or not at all. If you're not willing, just say so now, and –
WILLIE	I'll tell him, 'yes'.
MAGGIE	And truthfully?
WILLIE	Yes, Maggie. I'm resigned. You're growing on me, lass. I'll toe the line with you.

ALICE *and* VICKEY *enter in their Sunday clothes – the same at which Hobson grew indignant in Act One.*

ALICE	We're ready, Maggie.
MAGGIE	And time you were. It's not your weddings that you're dressing for. (*By trap*) Come up Tubby, and keep an eye on things.
VICKEY	(*to Will*) Will, have you got the ring?
MAGGIE	I have. Do you think I'd trust him to remember?

MAGGIE *goes off with* WILLIE. VICKEY *and* ALICE *are following, laughing.* TUBBY *comes up trap and throws old shoes after them.*

Either

1 Read the extract above. What do you think makes this an important and entertaining moment in the play? **(20 marks)**

Think about:

- what it tells us about Willie and Maggie's relationship

- how it changes things for the characters

- what it says about love and marriage.

or

2 In *Hobson's Choice*, how does the character of Willie change and develop throughout the play? **(20 marks)**

Remember to support your points with details from the play.

Score   / 20

How well did you do?

| 0–13 | Try again | 14–20 | Getting there | 21–27 | Good work | 28–35 | Excellent! |

For more information on this topic, see pages 54–55 of your *Success Revision Guide*.

Drama

Character and Audience

Multiple-choice questions

Choose just one answer: A, B, C or D.

1 What is a prop? **(1 mark)**
  - **A** Something that holds up the scenery.
  - **B** An object used on stage.
  - **C** An understudy.
  - **D** A type of light.

2 How could costume help our understanding of a character? **(1 mark)**
  - **A** By indicating his or her class and tastes.
  - **B** By making the production more colourful.
  - **C** By showing us when the play is set.
  - **D** By making the actor feel uncomfortable.

3 How can directions that describe lighting and sound help us? **(1 mark)**
  - **A** By indicating the kind of mood and atmosphere the playwright wants to create.
  - **B** By showing us exactly how the play should look.
  - **C** By making the play less boring to read.
  - **D** By showing us what is going on in the characters' minds.

4 What is meant by dramatic irony? **(1 mark)**
  - **A** Sarcasm.
  - **B** The audience knowing more than the characters do.
  - **C** Something that is not dramatic at all.
  - **D** Witty banter between the characters.

5 What is dialogue? **(1 mark)**
  - **A** All the words written by the playwright.
  - **B** Conversation between two characters.
  - **C** Conversation between two or more characters.
  - **D** Conversation between an actor and a member of the audience.

Score / 5

Short-answer questions

Read the passage on the right from the final act of J B Priestley's *An Inspector Calls*. Answer on a separate sheet of paper.

1 What impression do you get of the Inspector from this passage? **(2 marks)**

2 What does he mean by 'Eva Smiths and John Smiths'? **(2 marks)**

3 What do you think he is referring to when he mentions 'blood and fire and anguish'? Bear in mind that the play was set in 1912 but first performed in 1946. **(2 marks)**

4 How do you think the other characters might react to his words? **(2 marks)**

5 How do you think the audience might react? **(2 marks)**

> **INSPECTOR** (*turning at the door*) But just remember this. One Eva Smith has gone – but there are millions and millions of Eva Smiths and John Smiths still left with us, with their lives, their hopes and fears, their sufferings and chance of happiness, all intertwined with our lives, with what we think and say and do. We don't live alone. We are members of one body. We are responsible for each other. And I tell you that the time will soon come when, if men will not learn that lesson, then they will be taught it in fire and blood and anguish. Good night.

Score / 10

Continue on a separate sheet of paper if necessary.

An Inspector Calls

1 **Either**

a) How does Priestley present the character of Mr Birling in *An Inspector Calls?*   (10 marks)

or

b) 'We are responsible for each other.' What does *An Inspector Calls* have to say about moral and social responsibility?   (10 marks)

Kindertransport

2 **Either**

a) '*Kindertransport* is about how we can never escape our own history or the history of our world.'   (10 marks)

How far and in what ways do you agree with this view of the play?

or

b) Discuss the role and significance of the rat-catcher in *Kindertransport*.   (10 marks)

Drama

Score   / 20

How well did you do?

| 0–13 | Try again | 14–20 | Getting there | 21–27 | Good work | 28–35 | Excellent! |

For more information on this topic, see pages 56–57 of your Success Revision Guide.

Analysing a Moving Image

Multiple-choice questions

Choose just one answer: A, B, C or D.

1 The term 'mise-en-scene' refers to: (1 mark)
  A the scenery
  B the place where a film is set
  C everything that you see in the frame
  D the most important things on the set.

2 A connotation is: (1 mark)
  A something you can see
  B what something is used for
  C the implied meaning and associations of something you can see
  D the subtitles shown under a foreign-language film.

3 Non-diegetic sounds could include: (1 mark)
  A voice-overs or background music
  B any sound that seems out of place

  C sounds that create a realistic atmosphere
  D sounds made by the actors.

4 The likely connotation of the colour red is: (1 mark)
  A joy and happiness
  B doubt and uncertainty
  C danger and bloodshed
  D innocence and purity.

5 Which of the following is **not** a media text?   (1 mark)
  A A feature film.
  B An advertisement.
  C A reality television show.
  D A poem.

Score   / 5

Short-answer questions

1 Give five examples of diegetic sounds.   (5 marks)

2 Give five elements that make up a film's 'mise-en-scene'.   (5 marks)

Score   / 10

Continue on a separate sheet of paper if necessary.

Some exam boards encourage writing based on the moving image as part of the creative or imaginative writing unit in English Language.

Either

1 Write a review of a film you have seen recently. **(20 marks)**

Your review can be in the style of a broadsheet or tabloid newspaper, a teenage magazine or a specialist film magazine.

Make sure you write in an appropriate style for the chosen publication.

or

2 Write the opening scenes of a script for an episode of a soap opera that you enjoy. **(20 marks)**

Make sure that you describe the action as well as writing the dialogue.

Score   / 20

How well did you do?

| 0–13 | Try again | 14–20 | Getting there | 21–27 | Good work | 28–35 | Excellent! |

For more information on this topic, see pages 58–59 of your Success Revision Guide.

Analysing a Moving Image

Drama

Multiple-choice questions

Choose just one answer: A, B, C or D.

1 A close-up shot is often used to: **(1 mark)**
  A show a character's feelings
  B move in on a character
  C show us how old the character is
  D show us the relationship between two characters.

2 Interview shots can make the viewer feel like: **(1 mark)**
  A a neutral observer
  B a close friend
  C a passer-by
  D a suspect.

3 A low-angle shot can make a character appear: **(1 mark)**
  A lowly or subservient

  B shifty or unpleasant
  C powerful or superior
  D strange or mysterious.

4 A high-angle shot might make the viewer feel: **(1 mark)**
  A inferior
  B superior
  C indifferent
  D excited.

5 A tracking shot: **(1 mark)**
  A moves from one character to another
  B shows the whole scene
  C goes up and down with a character or object
  D follows a moving character or object.

Score / 5

Short-answer questions

Complete the following sentences using the correct technical terms. Give yourself two marks for each correct answer that is spelt correctly, or one mark for a close approximation.

1 During the opening sequence the camera _____ across the lakes and forests, quickly establishing the beauty and wildness of the setting. (2 marks)

2 The jerky movements of the _____ camera help to give us the feeling that it might have been shot by amateurs who happened upon a real-life incident. (2 marks)

3 Although they were considered advanced at the time, in this age of CGI, the movie's _____ appear clumsy and almost laughable. (2 marks)

4 Given that the scene begins with an _____ of the knife, it's pretty obvious that this object will play a significant part in the plot. (2 marks)

5 A series of rather dizzying _____ shots give us a bird's eye view of the chase, adding to the excitement. (2 marks)

Score / 10

Continue on a separate sheet of paper if necessary.

Some exam boards encourage candidates to write about versions of set texts made for television and cinemas.

Either

1 Write two contrasting reviews of a film adaptation of one of the texts you have studied this year.

Your reviews could be for a newspaper, a magazine or a website. Think carefully about the style of your chosen publication and its intended audience. **(20 marks)**

or

2 Compare two film or television adaptations of a text that you have studied this year.
You might wish to focus on two or three key scenes. **(20 marks)**

Score   / 20

Drama

How well did you do?

| 0–13 | Try again | 14–20 | Getting there | 21–27 | Good work | 28–35 | Excellent! |

For more information on this topic, see pages 60–61 of your Success Revision Guide.

Novels and Short Stories

Multiple-choice questions

Choose just one answer: A, B, C or D.

1 A novel is usually divided into: **(1 mark)**
- **A** stanzas
- **B** acts and scenes
- **C** movements
- **D** chapters.

2 Novels and short stories are types of: **(1 mark)**
- **A** non-fiction
- **B** fiction
- **C** persuasive writing
- **D** biographical writing.

3 Another name for a short novel is a: **(1 mark)**
- **A** novella
- **B** saga
- **C** long story
- **D** novelty.

4 Which of the following is **not** a contemporary writer? **(1 mark)**
- **A** Nick Hornby
- **B** Thomas Hardy
- **C** Susan Hill
- **D** Jacqueline Wilson

5 The opening chapter of a novel usually: **(1 mark)**
- **A** sets the scene, and introduces important characters and ideas
- **B** explains what the novel is all about
- **C** introduces all the characters and lists all their characteristics
- **D** tells us about the author.

Score / 5

Short-answer questions

1 See if you can find out the names of the authors of these five novels from the English literary heritage: **(6 marks)**

a) *Jane Eyre* ....

b) *Silas Marner* ....

c) *Vanity Fair* ....

d) *Pride and Prejudice* ....

e) *Animal Farm* ....

2 Explain what is meant by a 'cliffhanger'. **(2 marks)**

3 Explain what is meant by a 'protagonist'? **(2 marks)**

Score / 10

Continue on a separate piece of paper if necessary.

1 *Pride and Prejudice* (20 marks)

Answer both parts a) and b)

a) What impressions do you have of any **two** of the following characters:
Charlotte Lucas; Mr Bennet; Mrs Bennet; Mr Collins?
Remember to write about the society they live in.

b) How does Austen's way of writing create the characters you have chosen?

or

2 *The Withered Arm and Other Wessex Tales* (20 marks)

Answer both parts a) and b)

a) What impression do you get of the role of women from 'The Son's Veto'?
Remember to write about the society they live in.

b) How does Hardy's way of writing convey aspects of women's lives in **one** other story?

or

3 *Great Expectations* (20 marks)

Referring to **two** or **three** sections of the novel, show how Dickens creates tension and excitement.

Remember to write about the society in which the novel is set.

Prose

Score   / 20

How well did you do?

| 0–13 | Try again | 14–20 | Getting there | 21–27 | Good work | 28–35 | Excellent! |

For more information on this topic, see pages 64–65 of your Success Revision Guide.

Literary Techniques

Multiple-choice questions

Choose just one answer: A, B, C or D.

1 What is meant by 'diction'?   (1 mark)
- **A** The writer's choice of words.
- **B** The characters' accents.
- **C** The meaning of words.
- **D** The arrangement of words on the page.

2 What do we mean by the 'tone' of a novel?   (1 mark)
- **A** The quality of the descriptions in the text.
- **B** The kind of language the text is written in.
- **C** The feelings and actions of the character.
- **D** The overall feeling or attitude of the writing.

3 If the protagonist of a novel is also its narrator we would expect to be: (1 mark)
- **A** Less sympathetic towards him or her.
- **B** More sympathetic towards him or her.
- **C** Indifferent towards him or her.
- **D** Amused by him or her.

4 What should you do in order to gain high marks when discussing language?   (1 mark)
- **A** Remember that you can often interpret it in more than one way.
- **B** Give a precise definition of every word.
- **C** Use long words and complex sentences.
- **D** Work out exactly what the author intended you to think.

5 When quoting from a text you should always: (1 mark)
- **A** put the exact words from the original text within inverted commas
- **B** put the original text into your own words
- **C** write in capital letters
- **D** put the words taken from the text into brackets.

Score   / 5

Short-answer questions

The extract on the right is the opening of Thomas Hardy's story, *The Withered Arm*. Answer on a separate sheet of paper.

1 What does the passage tell you about the story's setting?   (2 marks)

2 What sort of life do you think the people in it lead?   (2 marks)

3 How would you describe the way they speak?   (2 marks)

4 How would you describe the general mood or atmosphere of the passage?   (2 marks)

5 Who do you think will be the main characters in the story?   (2 marks)

> It was an eighty-cow dairy, and the troop of milkers, regular and supernumerary, were all at work; for, though the time of year was as yet but early April, the feed lay entirely in the water meadows, and the cows were 'in full pail'. The hour was about six in the evening, and three-fourths of the large, red, rectangular animals having been finished off, there was opportunity for a little conversation.
>
> 'He do bring home his bride tomorrow, I hear. They've come as far as Anglebury today.'
>
> The voice seemed to proceed from the belly of a cow called Cherry, but the speaker was a milking woman, whose face was buried in the flank of that motionless beast.
>
> 'Hav' anybody seen her?' said another.

Score   / 10

Continue on a separate piece of paper if necessary.

A Christmas Carol

1 Read the following extract. Referring closely to the extract, show how Dickens presents the character of Scrooge. **(10 marks)**

> Oh! but he was a tight-fisted hand at the grindstone, clutching, covetous old sinner! Hard and sharp as flint, from which no steel had ever struck out generous fire; secret, and self-contained, and solitary as an oyster. The cold within him froze his old features, nipped his pointed nose, shrivelled his cheek, stiffened his gait; made his eyes red, his thin lips blue; and spoke out shrewdly in his grating voice. A frosty rime was on his head, and on his eyebrows, and his wiry chin. He carried his own low temperature always about him; he iced his office in the dog-days; and didn't thaw it one degree at Christmas.

and

2 **Either**

a) Discuss how Dickens uses this 'ghost story' to draw attention to the condition of the poor in Victorian England. **(10 marks)**

or

b) Show how Dickens uses each of the four ghosts to make changes to Scrooge's character. **(10 marks)**

Score / 20

How well did you do?

| 0–13 | Try again | | 14–20 | Getting there | | 21–27 | Good work | | 28–35 | Excellent! |

For more information on this topic, see pages 66–67 of your Success Revision Guide.

Exploring Culture in Prose

Multiple-choice questions

Choose just one answer: A, B, C or D.

1. Which of the following would **not** be considered part of someone's culture? **(1 mark)**
   - A Language
   - B Religion
   - C Music
   - D Age

2. If you study a text from a different culture, what language will it be in? **(1 mark)**
   - A French
   - B Punjabi
   - C Latin
   - D English

3. What is meant when a community is described as 'multicultural'? **(1 mark)**
   - A It includes people with many different cultural backgrounds.
   - B Only people from one cultural background can live there.
   - C There are lots of theatres, art galleries and museums.
   - D The people there have visited a lot of different countries.

4. Which of the following would we **not** consider as part of a text's cultural context? **(1 mark)**
   - A Where it is set.
   - B When it is set.
   - C What the language is like.
   - D How long it is.

5. What is meant by 'global' literature? **(1 mark)**
   - A Geography text books.
   - B Texts set in more than one country.
   - C Texts from anywhere in the world.
   - D Texts that have been translated into different languages.

Score / 5

Short-answer questions

The extract on the right is from Harper Lee's novel, *To Kill A Mockingbird*, written in 1960.

The novel is set in Alabama, USA in the 1930s. On a separate sheet of paper, answer the following questions, supporting each answer with a short quotation from the text.

1. What is your general impression of Maycomb? Is it prosperous or run down? **(2 marks)**

2. What impression do you get of the climate? **(2 marks)**

3. Which details indicate that the novel is set some time before it was written? **(2 marks)**

4. What impression do you get of the men of Maycomb? **(2 marks)**

5. What impression do you get of the women of Maycomb? **(2 marks)**

> Maycomb was an old town, but it was a tired old town when I first knew it. In rainy weather the streets turned to red slop; grass grew on the sidewalks, the courthouse sagged in the square. Somehow, it was hotter then: a black dog suffered on a summer's day; bony mules hitched to Hoover carts flicked flies in the sweltering shade of the live oaks on the square. Men's stiff collars wilted by nine in the morning. Ladies bathed before noon, after their three o'clock naps, and by nightfall were like soft tea-cakes with frostings of sweat and sweet talcum.

Score / 10

Continue on a separate piece of paper if necessary.

Make sure you divide your time equally between the two questions.

Read the passage from *To Kill a Mockingbird* and then answer the questions that follow.

> First Purchase African M.E. Church was in the Quarters outside the southern town limits, across the old sawmill tracks. It was an ancient paint-peeled frame building, the only church in Maycomb with a steeple and a bell, called First Purchase because it was paid for from the first earnings of freed slaves. Negroes worshipped in it on Sundays and white men gambled in it on weekdays.
>
> The churchyard was brick-hard clay, as was the cemetery beside it. If someone died during a dry spell, the body was covered with chunks of ice until rain softened the earth. A few graves in the cemetery were marked with crumbling tombstones; newer ones were outlined with brightly coloured glass and broken Coca-Cola bottles. Lightning rods guarding some graves denoted dead who rested uneasily. It was a happy cemetery.
>
> The warm bittersweet smell of clean Negro welcomed us as we entered the churchyard – hearts of Love hairdressing mingled with asafoetida, snuff, Hoyt's Cologne, Brown's Mule, peppermint, and lilac talcum.
>
> When they saw Jem and me with Calpurnia, the men stepped back and took off their hats; the women crossed their arms at their waists, weekday gestures of respectful attention. They parted and made a small pathway to the church door for us. Calpurnia walked between Jem and me, responding to the greetings of her brightly clad neighbours.
>
> 'What you up to, Miss Cal?' said a voice behind us.
>
> Calpurnia's hands went to our shoulders and we stopped and looked around; standing in the path behind us was a tall Negro woman. Her weight was on one leg; she rested her left elbow in the curve of her hip, pointing at us with upturned palm. She was bullet-headed with strange almond-shaped eyes, straight nose, and an Indian-bow mouth. She seemed seven feet high.
>
> I felt Calpurnia's hand dig into my shoulder. 'What you want, Lula?' she asked, in tones I had never heard her use. She spoke quietly, contemptuously.

1 How does the author use details in this passage to explore tensions between people from different ethnic groups? **(10 marks)**

....

....

....

and

2 What is the significance of Calpurnia in the novel as a whole? **(10 marks)**

....

....

....

....

Score / 20

How well did you do?

| 0–13 | Try again | 14–20 | Getting there | 21–27 | Good work | 28–35 | Excellent! |

For more information on this topic, see pages 68–69 of your Success Revision Guide.

Prose

Culture in *Of Mice and Men*

Multiple-choice questions

Choose just one answer: A, B, C or D.

1 Where is *Of Mice and Men* set? **(1 mark)**
   A New York
   B California
   C Ohio
   D Texas

2 When is *Of Mice and Men* set? **(1 mark)**
   A 1920s
   B 1930s
   C 1940s
   D 1950s

3 Where does the main action of the novel take place? **(1 mark)**
   A On a ranch.
   B In a factory.
   C On a mountain.
   D At sea.

4 Why do people in the novel look down on Crooks? **(1 mark)**
   A Because he is a man.
   B Because he is black.
   C Because he is Asian.
   D Because he is old.

5 Why might Steinbeck not have given Curley's wife a name? **(1 mark)**
   A Because she does not have one.
   B To show how important she is.
   C To make the reader guess what it is.
   D To show that she has a low status in society.

Score   / 5

Short-answer questions

What do the following quotations from *Of Mice and Men* tell you about the characters and their role in society? Answer on a separate sheet of paper. Give yourself up to two marks for each answer.

1 Lennie: (2 marks)

'Tried and tried,' said Lennie, 'but it didn't do no good. I remember about the rabbits, George.'

2 George: (2 marks)

'Now look – I'll give him the work tickets, but you ain't gonna say a word.'

3 Curley: (2 marks)

He glanced coldly at George and then at Lennie. His glance was at once calculating and pugnacious.

4 Curley's wife: (2 marks)

She had full, rouged lips and wide-spaced eyes, heavily made up...
Her voice had a nasal, brittle quality.

5 Crooks: (2 marks)

'You go on, get outa my room. I ain't wanted in the bunkhouse, and you ain't wanted in my room.'

Score   / 10

GCSE-style questions

Continue on a separate piece of paper if necessary.

Either

1 Read the following passage from *Of Mice and Men*.

> Then Curley's rage exploded. 'Come on, ya big bastard. Get up on your feet. No big son-of-a-bitch is gonna laugh at me. I'll show ya who's yella.'
>
> Lennie looked helplessly at George, and then he got up and tried to retreat. Curley was balanced and poised. He slashed at Lennie with his left, and then smashed down his nose with his right. Lennie gave a cry of terror. Blood welled from his nose. 'George,' he cried. 'Make 'um let me alone, George.' He backed until he was against the wall, and Curley followed, slugging him in the face. Lennie's hands remained at his sides; he was too frightened to defend himself.
>
> George was on his feet yelling,
> 'Get him, Lennie. Don't let him do it.'
>
> Lennie covered his face with his huge paws and bleated with terror. He cried, 'Make 'um stop, George.' Then Curley attacked his stomach and cut off his wind.
>
> Slim jumped up. 'The dirty little rat,' he cried, 'I'll get 'um myself.'
>
> George put out his hand and grabbed Slim, 'Wait a minute,' he shouted. He cupped his hands around his mouth and yelled, 'Get 'im, Lennie!'
>
> Lennie took his hands away from his face and looked about for George, and Curley slashed at his eyes. The big face was covered with blood. George yelled again, 'I said get him.'
>
> Curley's fist was swinging when Lennie reached for it. The next minute Curley was flopping like a fish on a line, and his closed fist was lost in Lennie's big hand. George ran down the room. 'Leggo of him, Lennie. Let go.'
>
> But Lennie watched in terror the flopping little man whom he held. Blood ran down Lennie's face, one of his eyes was cut and closed. George slapped him in the face again and again, and still Lennie held on to the closed fist.

How does Steinbeck's writing make this passage powerful and significant?

Focus on the writer's narrative style and use of language. **(20 marks)**

or

2 How does Steinbeck explore the experience of the Depression through the characters in *Of Mice and Men*? **(20 marks)**

Remember to support your points with details from the text.

Score   / 20

How well did you do?

| 0–13 | Try again | 14–20 | Getting there | 21–27 | Good work | 28–35 | Excellent! |

For more information on this topic, see pages 70–71 of your Success Revision Guide.

Poetic Form and Features

Multiple-choice questions

Choose just one answer: A, B, C or D.

1 Which of the following lines of poetry contains an example of alliteration? **(1 mark)**
  A He clasps the crag with crooked hands
  B Ringed with the azure world he stands
  C The wrinkled sea beneath him crawls
  D And like a thunderbolt he falls.

2 Which of the following lines contains an example of personification? **(1 mark)**
  A Swarms of minnows show their little heads
  B Their silver bellies on the pebbly sand
  C If anything might rouse him now
  D The kind old sun will know.

3 Which of the following lines contains an example of assonance? **(1 mark)**
  A All soft and still and fair
  B The silent time of midnight
  C Their breezy boughs on high
  D A shelter from the sky.

4 Which of the following lines contains a simile? **(1 mark)**
  A O, my luve's like a red, red rose
  B O mistress mine, where are you roaming?
  C Come live with me, and be my love
  D And we will sit upon the rocks.

5 Which of the following lines contains an internal rhyme? **(1 mark)**
  A The ant and the mole sit both in a hole
  B And frog peeps out o' the fountain
  C Upon the gale she stooped her side
  D And bounded o'er the swelling tide.

Score / 5

Short-answer questions

Which of the following statements apply to:

  a) a sonnet   **b)** a ballad   **c)** free verse?

Give yourself one mark for each correct answer.

1 It has fourteen lines. .... (1 mark)

2 It tells a story. .... (1 mark)

3 It does not rhyme. .... (1 mark)

4 It is arranged in stanzas. .... (1 mark)

5 It is written in iambic pentameter. .... (1 mark)

6 It is usually about love. .... (1 mark)

7 Usually, the second and fourth lines rhyme. .... (1 mark)

8 It can be either Shakespearean or Petrachan. .... (1 mark)

9 It does not have a regular metre or rhythm. .... (1 mark)

10 Most modern poetry is written in it. .... (1 mark)

Score / 10

GCSE-style questions

Continue on a separate piece of paper if necessary.

Unseen Poetry

Read the poem below, *She Dwelt among the Untrodden Ways* by William Wordsworth.
Answer **both** questions that follow.

> She dwelt among the untrodden ways
>   Beside the springs of Dove*,
> A Maid whom there were none to praise
>   And very few to love:
>
> A violet by a mossy stone
>   Half hidden from the eye!
> —Fair as a star, when only one
>   Is shining in the sky.
>
> She lived unknown, and few could know
>   When Lucy ceased to be;
> But she is in her grave, and, oh,
>   The difference to me!
>
> * The Dove is a river in the English Lake
> District

1 What is the speaker saying about Lucy and his feelings for her?   (10 marks)

and

2 How does the poet present Lucy and his feelings about her through the way in which he describes them?   (10 marks)

Score   / 20

How well did you do?

| 0–13 | Try again | 14–20 | Getting there | 21–27 | Good work | 28–35 | Excellent! |

For more information on this topic, see pages 74–75 of your Success Revision Guide.

Poetry Comparison

Multiple-choice questions

Choose just one answer: A, B, C or D.

1 If you are asked to write about 'unseen poetry' what will you be writing about? **(1 mark)**
  A Poetry that has never been written down.
  B Poetry that nobody has ever seen before.
  C Poetry that you have not seen and studied.
  D Poetry that does not rhyme.

2 Which of the following words and phrases would you **not** use when discussing the differences between poems? **(1 mark)**
  A Similarly
  B Whereas
  C On the other hand
  D In contrast

3 Which of the following words and phrases would you **not** use when discussing the similarities between poems? **(1 mark)**

  A Likewise
  B In the same way
  C Both... and
  D However

4 When writing about poetry you should always: **(1 mark)**
  A discuss your personal response
  B write in black ink
  C discuss the poet's life.
  D write about as many poems as you can.

5 When writing about poetry you should refer to the writer either by his or her surname or as: **(1 mark)**
  A the playwright
  B whatever his or her first name is
  C the poet
  D the versifier.

Score   / 5

Poetry

Short-answer questions

Read the poem below, *The Eagle* by Alfred Lord Tennyson. Answer the questions that follow, giving yourself up to two marks for each. Continue on a separate sheet of paper.

1 What would you say were the main themes of the poem? **(2 marks)**

> He clasps the crag with crooked hands;
> Close to the sun in lonely lands,
> Ringed with the azure world, he stands.
>
> The wrinkled sea beneath him crawls;
> He watches from his mountain walls,
> And like a thunderbolt he falls.

2 What happens in the poem? **(2 marks)**

3 How does Tennyson's language make the eagle seem like a human? **(2 marks)**

4 What effect does the use of alliteration in the first line have? **(2 marks)**

5 What effect does the simile in the last line have? **(2 marks)**

Score   / 10

Continue on a separate piece of paper if necessary.

There is a wide choice of collections of poetry available for study at GCSE. Usually, an exam question will name at least one of the poems you should write about. However, as it is unlikely that you would have studied any poems that we chose to name, the following questions are not specific to particular poems. You should be able to use poems that you have studied in answering at least one of them.

Either

1 Compare the way in which character and voice are presented in two poems that you have studied. **(20 marks)**

or

2 Compare the way in which two poets write about love and relationships. **(20 marks)**

or

3 Compare the treatment of war in two poems that you have studied. **(20 marks)**

or

4 Show how a poet whom you have studied uses imagery to express his or her feelings. **(20 marks)**

or

5 Write about the ways in which a poet whom you have studied writes about the natural world. **(20 marks)**

Poetry

Score   / 20

How well did you do?

| 0–13 | Try again | 14–20 | Getting there | 21–27 | Good work | 28–35 | Excellent! |

For more information on this topic, see pages 76–77 of your Success Revision Guide.

Presenting Information and Ideas

Multiple-choice questions

Choose just one answer: A, B, C or D.

1 What is meant by an individual presentation? **(1 mark)**
A A presentation you do only once.
B An unusual or eccentric speech.
C A presentation or speech that you do alone.
D A presentation with only one person listening.

2 When making a formal speech what sort of language should you use? **(1 mark)**
A Slang
B Standard English
C Non-standard English
D Welsh

3 When making your speech you should: **(1 mark)**
A read from your notes
B make eye contact with your audience
C walk around the room
D stop every now and again to ask how you are doing.

4 Which of the following is **not** an example of a rhetorical device that you could use in a speech? **(1 mark)**
A Rhetorical question
B List of three
C Hyperbole
D Anticlimax

5 What should you do in response to questions from the audience? **(1 mark)**
A Ignore them.
B Answer them as briefly as possible.
C Answer them fully, using the opportunity to develop your ideas.
D Ask the teacher to answer them.

Score / 5

Short-answer questions

1 Below is a series of prompt-card notes for a talk about someone's hobby. Put them in order. (5 marks)

a) Some of the basic rules and moves.

b) How I got into it – where I do it – when I do it.

c) What is taekwando and what are its origins?

d) What does the future hold for me and the sport?

e) Why I like it.

2 Here are some prompts for a speech appealing for support for a local charity. Put them in order. (5 marks)

a) Why I am here – and what is the charity?

b) Focus on the Bashumi village project (clips of village life). Why they need help.

c) What can you do to help?

d) What has been achieved by the charity and what more needs to be done (digging wells).

e) More details of their work – an overview around the world.

Score / 10

GCSE-style questions

The tasks on this page and on page 67 are suitable for GCSE controlled assessments.

Plan your presentation and, if possible, perform it in front of friends or family and ask them to assess you. Alternatively, you could record your presentation, play it back and mark yourself.

Continue on a separate sheet of paper if necessary.

Individual Presentations

1 Give a talk, lasting about five minutes, to a group of fellow pupils about a hobby or interest that you enjoy.   **(20 marks)**

or

2 Give a presentation to your class, based on your own research, on the life and work of a writer you have studied and whose work you enjoy.   **(20 marks)**

or

3 Talk for five minutes about an interesting place that you have visited, informing your audience about the attractions of the place, and saying what it means to you.   **(20 marks)**

Score   / 20

How well did you do?

| 0–13 | Try again | 14–20 | Getting there | 21–27 | Good work | 28–35 | Excellent! |

For more information on this topic, see pages 80–81 of your Success Revision Guide.

Speaking and Listening

Group Discussion and Drama

Multiple-choice questions

Choose just one answer: A, B, C or D.

1 Which of the following is important in group discussion? **(1 mark)**
 A Having the last word.
 B Listening to others and building on their points.
 C Saying more than anyone else.
 D Smiling and nodding a lot.

2 Which of these is an example of an open question? **(1 mark)**
 A How old are you?
 B Do you like ice cream?
 C How many fingers am I holding up?
 D Why do you think young people turn to drugs?

3 In a drama-based exercise which of these is important? **(1 mark)**
 A Staying in role.
 B Being yourself.
 C Looking nice.
 D Using long words.

4 What is meant by a character's motivation? **(1 mark)**
 A His or her personality.
 B His or her position in life.
 C What make him or her act in a certain way.
 D The reason the writer created him or her.

5 During a drama-based exercise you should: **(1 mark)**
 A read from a script
 B remain completely still
 C think about body language and facial expressions
 D sit with your back to the audience.

Score / 5

Short-answer questions

For your controlled assessments, you must do three different kinds of speaking and listening assignment:

a) an individual presentation **b)** a drama-based activity **c)** a group discussion.

Match the following assignments to the correct activity.

1 An improvisation based on a poem you have read in class. (1 mark)

2 A class debate about gang crime in your local area. (1 mark)

3 A mock interview for a job as an astronaut. (1 mark)

4 A talk about your favourite sport. (1 mark)

5 A discussion about school uniform in a group of four. (1 mark)

6 A presentation to the class about your favourite songs, illustrated by video and audio clips. (1 mark)

7 A formal speech appealing for funds for a charity. (1 mark)

8 A 'Jeremy Kyle' type chat show based on the characters in *Macbeth*. (1 mark)

9 A formal debate with the title 'Should we close down our nuclear power stations?' (1 mark)

10 A pair activity in which each person plays a character from history. (1 mark)

1 .... 2 .... 3 .... 4 .... 5 .... 6 .... 7 .... 8 .... 9 .... 10 ....

Score / 10

These tasks are suitable for GCSE controlled assessments.

Plan your chosen tasks and, if possible, get together with a group of fellow pupils to do them. You could then peer-assess the work. Alternatively, you could record your presentation, play it back and mark yourself.

Group Discussion

1 Many people are very concerned by an increase in knife and gun crime locally. Others say that there is nothing to worry about and the problem has been blown out of all proportion. What do you think? **(20 marks)**

or

2 You have been asked to review your school's dress code. You may **either**: **(20 marks)**

 a) retain the current uniform or

 b) change the uniform or

 c) abolish uniform altogether.

 Discuss these three possibilities.

Drama-based Activities

1 With a partner, choose two characters from a text you have been studying. Take turns at interviewing the characters for a local television show. **(20 marks)**

or

2 In a small group, perform an improvisation showing what you think would have happened if you and your colleagues had been taken hostage during your work experience placement. **(20 marks)**

Speaking and Listening

Score   / 40

How well did you do?

| 0–19 | Try again | 20–29 | Getting there | 30–40 | Good work | 41–55 | Excellent! |

For more information on this topic, see pages 82–83 of your Success Revision Guide.

Studying Spoken Language

Multiple-choice questions

Choose just one answer: A, B, C or D.

1 What is an idiolect? **(1 mark)**
  A A way of speaking that sounds silly.
  B An individual's way of speaking.
  C A regional variation of speech.
  D The wrong way to speak.

2 What do accents tell us about people? **(1 mark)**
  A How old they are.
  B Whether they are male or female.
  C Where they come from.
  D Whether or not they like us.

3 Which of the following is an example of a formal greeting? **(1 mark)**
  A All right, mate.
  B Hiya, babe.
  C Hello, my darling.
  D Good evening, sir.

4 Which of the following is an example of a paralinguistic feature? **(1 mark)**
  A Scratching your nose.
  B A tape recording.
  C Using a lot of adverbs.
  D Using dialect words.

5 What do we call a written record of speech? **(1 mark)**
  A A thesis.
  B A thesaurus.
  C A transmogrification.
  D A transcript.

Score   / 5

Short-answer questions

The following statements are not in Standard English. Re-write them so that they sound more formal. Give yourself up to two marks for each answer.

1 I was like dead into nursing and that, so I did me work experience in a hospital. **(2 marks)**

....

2 If you ask me, the police don't know nothing about gangs. **(2 marks)**

....

3 He turned round and said, 'You've got it all wrong', so I'm like, 'What does he mean?' **(2 marks)**

....

4 Ain't no mountain high enough, ain't no river deep enough, to keep me from you. **(2 marks)**

....

5 Nay, I'd be feared to go in them fine places. **(2 marks)**

....

Score   / 10

GCSE-style questions

The study of spoken language is always tested by means of controlled assessment. These are examples of tasks suitable for GCSE controlled assessments.

Either

❶ A study of a particular speaker   (20 marks)

Choose a well-known public figure, for example a politician or a comedian, and record a speech or monologue.

In your study you should look at:

• how the speech is structured and its key features
• how the speaker connects to the audience
• how language is used (e.g. diction, register, rhetorical devices) to create an impact
• the use of paralinguistic features (e.g. body language, pausing, tone of voice).

or

❷ A study of how language is used by staff in a fast food restaurant   (20 marks)

Study speech both between staff members and between staff and customers.

In your study you should look at:

• the register and diction used
• how information is shared
• how instructions and requests are given and received
• turn-taking and non-verbal interjections
• the influence of context on language choices.

Score   / 20

How well did you do?

| 0–13 | Try again | 14–20 | Getting there | 21–27 | Good work | 28–35 | Excellent! |

For more information on this topic, see pages 84–85 of your Success Revision Guide.

Studying Spoken Language

Multiple-choice questions

Choose just one answer: A, B, C or D.

1 What is meant by 'code switching'? **(1 mark)**
- **A** Changing the way you talk according to circumstances.
- **B** Speaking in a foreign language.
- **C** Changing your telephone number.
- **D** Taking turns speaking.

2 In which of these situations would speech **not** have been consciously crafted? **(1 mark)**
- **A** An interview between a television presenter and a politician.
- **B** A school assembly.
- **C** A presentation at conference.
- **D** A conversation with your next-door neighbour.

3 Which of these is an example of 'muti-modal talk'? **(1 mark)**
- **A** Making a speech.
- **B** Having a group discussion.
- **C** Showing a DVD.
- **D** Texting.

4 Which of these is an example of phonetic spelling? **(1 mark)**
- **A** TMB
- **B** KT iz gr8
- **C** See you later
- **D** :-)

5 A common criticism of texting is that: **(1 mark)**
- **A** it takes too long
- **B** it costs too much
- **C** you need to be very good at English
- **D** it encourages poor spelling and grammar.

Score   / 5

Short-answer questions

Briefly explain what each of the symbols represents in a transcript of speech.

1 (.) .... (1 mark)

2 (3) .... (1 mark)

3 // .... (1 mark)

Which features of spontaneous speech can you identify?

4 You <u>gonna</u> go down the market later? (1 mark)

....

5 I <u>er</u> don't really want to say. (1 mark)

....

Score   / 5

GCSE-style questions

The study of spoken language is always tested by means of controlled assessment. These are examples of tasks suitable for GCSE controlled assessments.

Either

1 Listen to a variety of examples of public speaking. Show your understanding of how and why language changes. **(20 marks)**

You can refer to:

- how language is used for a variety of purposes
- the importance of language choices
- regional and non-standard variations in speech
- variations in speech due to context and audience.

or

2 Listen to a variety of acts by stand-up comedians. **(20 marks)**

Show your understanding of how and why language changes.

You can refer to:

- how language is used for a variety of purpose
- the importance of language choices
- regional and non-standard variations in speech
- variations in speech due to context and audience.

Score / 20

How well did you do?

| 0–10 | Try again | 11–17 | Getting there | 18–24 | Good work | 25–30 | Excellent! |

For more information on this topic, see pages 86–87 of your Success Revision Guide.

Mixed GCSE-Style Questions

Reading Non-Fiction

Write your answers on a separate sheet of paper.

Look back at the three non-fiction texts: 'Lake Garda' on page 11, 'Courage is Timeless' on page 13, and 'Yasha, 8, Is Sum Genius' on page 15.

First, read the passage 'Lake Garda' on page 11.

1 According to this passage, why is Lake Garda worth visiting? **(5 marks)**

2 How does the writer use language to make Lake Garda seem attractive to the reader? **(5 marks)**

Now read 'Courage is Timeless' on page 13.

3 Why, according to the article, should people leave money to the RNLI in their wills? **(5 marks)**

4 What sort of people do you think the article would appeal to? Give reasons for your answer. **(5 marks)**

Now read 'Yasha, 8, Is Sum Genius' on page 15 and 'Courage Is Timeless' together.

5 Compare the attitudes of the writers to the people they are writing about. **(10 marks)**

6 Compare the ways in which the two articles are presented. You might consider: **(10 marks)**

- the use of headlines and sub-headings
- the use of fonts
- the use of any other presentational devices (e.g. images or photographs).

Functional Writing

Write your answers on a separate sheet of paper.

Either

1 You have been invited to give a talk to a group of Year Six pupils at a local primary school, informing them about what to expect when they come to your school next September.

Write a short script for your talk. **(20 marks)**

or

2 You have become involved in a campaign to preserve a piece of local woodland, well known as a habitat for wildlife, from being developed by a supermarket chain. You have been asked to write the text for a leaflet that will be delivered to local homes.

Write the text for the leaflet. **(20 marks)**

or

3 You have become concerned about the amount of litter on the pavement outside your house and the graffiti on local buildings. Last year your newly elected councillor promised to 'clean up' the area, but it has only got worse. You have decided to write to him or her about the problem.

Write your letter. **(20 marks)**

or

4 Your grandmother has been asked to provide one of her recipes for a book of traditional dishes being sold in aid of a local charity. The charity wants the recipes to be accompanied by stories about their origins. Because she cannot see very well, your grandmother has asked you to write it for her.

Write the recipe and its story. **(20 marks)**

or

5 You have recently returned from a tour abroad, as part of a regional sports team. Your head teacher has asked you to write a report for the school website.

Write your report. **(20 marks)**

or

6 You have seen a magazine article about a new programme on television that is looking for 12 teenagers from across the country to take part in an expedition to the North Pole. To apply, you must write a letter telling the producers about yourself and saying why they should pick you.

Write your letter of application. **(20 marks)**

Mixed GCSE-Style Questions

Creative/Imaginative Writing

Write your answers on a separate sheet of paper.

Narrative Writing

Either

❶ Write the opening of a story about a character who is the only survivor of a plane crash on a remote island in the Pacific Ocean.   **(20 marks)**

or

❷ Write a story that starts: 'If only I had remembered to top-up my phone...'   **(20 marks)**

Descriptive Writing

Either

❶ Write a description of your ideal home.   **(20 marks)**

or

❷ Describe a person you have met a few times but do not know well. Explain why this person interests you.   **(20 marks)**

Personal Writing

Either

❶ Write about an event in your early childhood that had a significant effect on you.   **(20 marks)**

or

❷ What do you like and dislike about your best friend?   **(20 marks)**

Re-creative Writing

Either

❶ Imagine that you have been transported to the world of the Shakespeare play you have studied, and you meet one of the main characters. Describe your encounter.   **(20 marks)**

or

❷ Write a new ending to one of the novels or stories you have studied.   **(20 marks)**

Shakespeare

Write your answers on a separate sheet of paper.

1 *Twelfth Night*

Answer both parts **a)** and **b)**.

a) How does Shakespeare show Orsino's feelings in the extract below?　　**(10 marks)**
In your answer you should write about:

- what Orsino's thoughts and feelings are

- how Shakespeare shows his thoughts and feelings through the way he writes.

b) Write about Orsino's thoughts and feelings in another part of the play.　　**(10 marks)**

> **ORSINO**　If music be the food of love, play on.
> Give me excess of it, that, surfeiting,
> The appetite may sicken, and so die.
> That strain again, it had a dying fall:
> O, it came o'er my ear like the sweet sound
> That breathes upon a bank of violets,
> Stealing and giving odour. Enough, no more;
> 'Tis not so sweet now as it was before.
> O spirit of love, how quick and fresh art thou,
> That notwithstanding thy capacity
> Receiveth as the sea, nought enters there,
> Of what validity and pitch soe'er,
> But falls into abatement and low price
> Even in a minute! So full of shapes is fancy,
> That it alone is high fantastical.
>
> **CURIO**　Will you go hunt, my lord?
>
> **ORSINO**　What, Curio?
>
> **CURIO**　The hart.
>
> **ORSINO**　Why so I do, the noblest that I have.

2 *Much Ado About Nothing*

Either

a) Why does Beatrice tell Benedick to kill Claudio?　　**(20 marks)**

or

b) Show how Shakespeare presents the character of Hero throughout the play.　　**(20 marks)**

Mixed GCSE-Style Questions

Drama

Write your answers on a separate sheet of paper.

1 *An Inspector Calls*

Either

a) What do we learn about Eva Smith throughout the play, and what is her significance? **(20 marks)**

or

b) Why do you think Priestley chose to set his play in an upper-middle-class household before World War I? **(20 marks)**

2 *The Crucible*

Either

a) How does Miller make the story of the Salem witches relevant to present-day audiences? **(20 marks)**

or

b) How does the character of John Proctor develop and change during the play? **(20 marks)**

3 *Educating Rita*

Either

a) What, if anything, does the play have to say about education? **(20 marks)**

or

b) Discuss the importance of two or three characters who are mentioned but never seen on stage. **(20 marks)**

4 *Under Milk Wood*

Either

a) It has been said that Llaregub is itself a character in *Under Milk Wood*. How far and in what ways would you agree with that view? **(20 marks)**

or

b) What does the character of the Reverend Eli Jenkins contribute to the play? **(20 marks)**

5 *Blood Brothers*

Either

a) How effective do you find the beginning of *Blood Brothers*? **(20 marks)**

or

b) Discuss the character and significance of Linda. **(20 marks)**

6 *A Taste of Honey*

Either

a) Do you find the character of Jo a convincing portrayal of a teenage girl? **(20 marks)**

or

b) How effective do you find the ending of *A Taste of Honey*? **(20 marks)**

Prose

Write your answers on a separate piece of paper.

1 Chimamanda Ngozi Adichie, *Purple Hibiscus* **(20 marks)**

Read the passage below and then answer the questions that follow.

'Look at this,' Papa-Nnukwu said. 'This is a woman spirit, and the women mmuo are harmless. They do not even go near the big ones at the festival.' The mmuo he pointed to was small; its carved wooden face had angular, pretty features and rouged lips. It stopped often to dance, wiggling this way and that, so the string of beads around its waist swayed and rippled. The crowds near by cheered, and some people threw money toward it. Little boys – the followers of the mmuo who were playing music with metal ogenes and wooden ichakasa – picked up the crumpled naira notes. They had hardly passed us when Papa Nnukwu shouted, 'Look away! Women cannot look at this one!'

The mmuo making its way down the road was surrounded by a few elderly men who rang a shrill bell as the mmuo walked. Its mask was a real, grimacing human skull with sunken eyes sockets. A squirming tortoise was tied to its forehead. A snake and three dead chickens hung from its grass-covered body, swinging as the mmuo walked. The crowds near the road moved back quickly, fearfully. A few women turned and dashed into nearby compounds.

Aunty Ifeoma looked amused, but she turned her head away. 'Don't look, girls. Let's humour your grandfather,' she said in English. Amaka has already looked away, too, toward the crowd of people that pressed around the car. It was sinful, deferring to a heathen masquerade. But at the least I had looked at it very briefly, so maybe it would technically not be deferring to a heathen masquerade.

'That is our *agwonatumbe*,' Papa-Nnnukwu said, proudly, after the mmuo had walked past. 'It is the most powerful mmuo in our parts, and all the neighbouring villages fear Abba because of it. At last year's Aro festival, *agwonatumbe* raised a staff and all the other mmuo turned and ran! They didn't even wait to see what would happen!'

a) In this passage, how does Adichie show attitudes towards traditional beliefs in Nigeria? Refer closely to the text.

and

b) How are attitudes towards traditional beliefs presented in the novel as a whole?

2 *The AQA Anthology* **(20 marks)**

a) What do you think is the importance of the setting of *When the Wasps Drowned*?

and

b) Go on to write about the setting of one other story from the anthology and how effective you find it.

3 *Martyn Pig* **(20 marks)**

How does Kevin Brooks build tension and create a sense of mystery in *Martyn Pig*?

4 *The Woman in Black* **(20 marks)**

How does Arthur Kipps change and develop as a result of his experience at Eel Marsh House?

Prose

5 *Lord of the Flies* **(20 marks)**

'*Lord of the Flies* is a frightening novel because it tells the truth about children'. How far and in what ways do you agree with this statement?

6 *Animal Farm* **(20 marks)**

What is the importance of Boxer in *Animal Farm*?

7 *Silas Marner* **(20 marks)**

How does Eliot present Silas Marner as a character with whom the reader may sympathise?

8 *Great Expectations* **(20 marks)**

What does Pip learn from his encounters with any **two** of the following characters: Miss Havisham; Joe Gargery; Mr Wopsle; Herbert Pocket; Mr Jaggers?

9 *Wuthering Heights* **(20 marks)**

What do you think is the point of the 'second generation' of characters in *Wuthering Heights*?

10 *Pride and Prejudice* **(20 marks)**

What does the experience of the Bennet sisters tell you about the relative importance of love and money?

Poetry: Writing about Unseen Poetry

Write your answers on a separate piece of paper.

In the first of the following poems, *The Thrush's Nest,* Clare describes how he watched a thrush making her nest, laying eggs and, at last, the chicks flying from the nest. In the second, *The Tyger,* Blake writes about the power of the tiger and wonders whether the God who made the gentle lamb could also have made this animal.

Write about the poems and your response to them. Write about their similarities and their differences.

You should include some or all of these points:

- the content of the poems
- the ideas the poets may want us to think about
- the mood or atmosphere of the poems
- how they are written – language that you find interesting, the way they are organised, etc.
- your personal responses.

(20 marks)

The Thrush's Nest

Within a thick and spreading hawthorn bush,
That overhung a molehill large and round,
I heard from morn to morn a merry thrush
Sing hymns to sunrise, and I drank the sound
With joy; and, often an intruding guest,
I watched her secret toils from day to day –
How true she warped the moss, to form a nest,
And modelled it within with wood and clay;
And by and by, like heath-bells gilt with dew,
There lay her shining eggs as bright as flowers,
Ink-spotted over shells of greeny blue:
And there I witnessed in the sunny hours
A brood of nature's minstrels chirp and fly,
Glad as that sunshine and the laughing sky.

John Clare

The Tyger

Tyger! Tyger! burning bright
In the forests of the night,
What immortal hand or eye
Could frame thy fearful symmetry?

In what distant deeps or skies
Burned the fire of thine eyes?
On what wings dare he aspire?
What the hand dare seize the fire?

And what shoulder, and what art,
Could twist the sinews of thy heart?
And when thy heart began to beat
What dread hand? And what dread feet?

What the hammer? What the chain?
In what furnace was thy brain?
What the anvil? What dread grasp
Dare its deadly terrors clasp?

When the stars threw down their spears,
And water'd heaven with their tears,
Did he smile his work to see?
Did he who made the Lamb make thee?

Tyger! Tyger! burning bright
In the forests of the night,
What immortal hand or eye
Dare frame they fearful symmetry?

William Blake

Notes